FENG SHUI

THE CHINESE ART OF
DESIGNING A HARMONIOUS ENVIRONMENT

DEREK WALTERS

A FIRESIDE BOOK
PUBLISHED BY SIMON & SCHUSTER INC.
NEW YORK – LONDON – TORONTO – SYDNEY – TOKYO

THE AUTHOR

Derek Walters, one of the few experts on Chinese astrology in the Western hemisphere, has also extended his research to the first-hand study of *Feng Shui*, working with several practising geomancers in the Far East. His adaptation of the *Lo P'an* – the geomancer's compass – to the format featured in this book is a remarkable achievement, enabling the reader unfamiliar with written Chinese to make accurate *Feng Shui* calculations for the very first time.

A Fireside Book
Published by Simon & Schuster Inc.
Simon & Schuster Building
Rockefeller Center
1230 Avenue of the Americas
New York, New York 10020

FIRESIDE and colophon are registered trademarks
of Simon & Schuster Inc.

Originally published in 1988 in Great Britain
by Pagoda Books, London

Printed and bound in U.K.

1   3   5   7   9   10   8   6   4   2

Library of Congress Cataloging in Publication Data

Walters, Derek, 1936-
    Feng Shui.
    "A Fireside book."
    Includes index.
    1. Feng-shui.   I. Title.
BF1779.F4W27   1988   133.3'33   88-4515
ISBN 0-671-66790-4

Contents

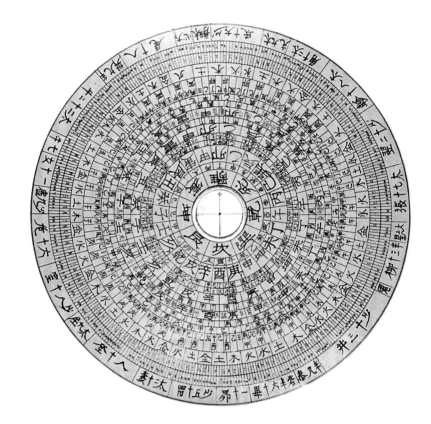

The Plates

Introduction

A complex blend of sound commonsense, fine aesthetics, and mystical philosophy, *Feng Shui* is a traditional Chinese technique which aims to ensure that all things are in harmony with their surroundings. Its application ranges from the planning of entire cities to the placing of a single flower in a vase, from the orientation of high-rise office blocks to the interior furnishing of a humble studio apartment. What we might refer to as the 'feel' of a place – good or bad – is called by the Chinese its *Feng Shui*. Unlike Westerners, however, the Chinese will often be able to give sound reasons why a particular spot should give an impression of peace, or of unease. Having the correct *Feng Shui* in the home, for instance, is said to enhance happiness and prosperity. Certainly, if the interior is pleasing, this will promote tranquillity, and it is easy to understand how this might lead to increased confidence and success.

There can be no exact translation of *Feng Shui* (rhyme *Feng* with 'tongue' and *Shui* with 'sway'), since it has no true equivalent in Western terms. The words themselves mean 'wind' and 'water': both wind and water 'flow', and this gives some clue to the nature of *Feng Shui*. Remarkably, the theory that there were currents of invisible energy which flowed in certain directions was firmly established in Chinese philosophy centuries before the discovery of the Earth's magnetism. Long before 'lines of force' became the backbone of school-book physics, lines of beneficial and malign currents were integral to the study of *Feng Shui*, and known respectively as *ch'i* and *sha*. *Ch'i* currents are understood to meander gently along irregular paths, while *sha* strike viciously in straight lines. Curved surfaces favour the advantageous *ch'i*; sharp edges, the harmful *sha*. Modern researchers have drawn parallels between the *ch'i* and *sha* currents and the Western concept of ley lines: but though they are in some ways analogous, they are not wholly similar. And whatever cosmic forces may be manifested in ley lines, if for evil, they are not held in the same abhorrence that the Chinese reserve for the malevolent forces known as the 'secret arrows' of *Feng Shui*.

The term *ch'i* was also used by the astronomers of old to describe mysterious meteorological phenomena that have never been positively identified: and it is the same term that is still used today by acupuncturists to describe the flow of vital energies in the body. Though these currents are not identical, it is an intuitive aspect of Chinese philosophy that the features of Heaven and Earth are also to be found in the human frame.

The origins of Feng Shui

The province of Kuang-hsi, in South-West China, is one of the most spectacularly scenic regions in the world. Its fantastically shaped hills and meandering rivers have been celebrated by Chinese painters and poets for centuries; and it was here, in the ninth century, that the scholar Yang Yün-sung was inspired to compile the first systematic approach to the study of the Form school of *Feng Shui*, its principles based for the most part on influences produced by the undulations of the landscape and tortuous routes taken by streams and water-courses.

Yang Yün-sung declared that the best location for a settlement would be on the side of a South-facing hill, with a pool of water at the foot. At first glance, this may merely seem to be a case of stating the obvious: the mountains would be a protection from wind and hostile attack; the Southern aspect would provide light and warmth; and the water would be vital to sustain the inhabitants. But further reasoning reveals that Yang Yün-sung must have had considerations other than plain commonsense: the side of a hill may not be such a good defensive position as the top, and flowing water is probably preferable to a stagnant pond.

A century after Yang Yün-sung had compiled his treatises, *Feng Shui* scholars in the North became concerned that the Form theory was too subjective. Much more academic in their approach, these later scholars placed greater emphasis on the importance of precise mathematical calculations, and compiled elaborate formulae and schematic diagrams – theories which took into account every conceivable directional, astronomical and calendrical implication. The 'Compass' theory which they formulated thus embraced some of the oldest and also very newest ideas.

The Compass school asserted that certain directions exert greater or lesser beneficial influences at particular times for specific events. The South, for example, is traditionally associated with the Summer season, and the Element Fire; but whether or not it would be auspicious to build in that direction would depend a great deal on the building's ultimate function.

The fundamental importance attached to the points of the compass is actually older than the invention of writing, a fact which can be ascertained from folk-lore and oral traditions. By the time of Confucius (551-479 BC), an elaborate ritual dictated the location and direction of the apartments which the Emperor would occupy at different times of the year, so that his actions would be in accordance with Heaven's movements. Centuries later, when China began to evolve as an empire, its capital cities were aligned with the cardinal points so that they would be a model of the Great Plan, and Heaven and Earth would

A late Ch'ing representation of the selection of the site for the future city of Lo-Yang.

be in harmony. At the centre of the city – and so, the heart of the Universe – was the palace, a miniature city in itself; and at the hub of the palace sat the Emperor, facing South, this being the most auspicious direction of all.

But although both schools of *Feng Shui* reflect very ancient traditions, as shown by passages in the Classics, particularly the intriguing stories of diviners and mystics attached to the official 'Histories' of the early Dynasties, no detailed methods of *Feng Shui* were described until the ninth or tenth centuries.

The contours of hills which surround any given location ideally form shapes known as the 'Dragon' and 'Tiger': and when these two forms are perfectly harmonious, the resulting *Feng Shui* traditionally ensures the peace and prosperity of the region. Perhaps not surprisingly, therefore, the impact of the Industrial Revolution was to bring considerable anxiety for the general populace. Railways sliced through the veins

of benevolent 'Dragons', and straight rails created paths for 'secret arrows' and thus unfavourable *Feng Shui*. Objections to the destruction of the local *Feng Shui* – protected by law – were made at every stage; and this resistance to any possible endangering of the *Feng Shui* is in fact one of the principal reasons for China's railway system being notoriously under strength.

But in many ways, such insistence that the existing *Feng Shui* had to be protected, though frequently derided as a barrier to progress, was not completely negative. In fact, in the Western hemisphere, it is only within recent years that conservation has been taken seriously, so that it is no longer thought suitable for unsightly cables to festoon the countryside, or for new buildings, whether residential or industrial, to disfigure the landscape – all of which, as the Chinese have been saying repeatedly, destroy the favourable *Feng Shui*.

Feng Shui today

It is generally supposed that since the Cultural Revolution in China, 'superstitious' practices have been eradicated. This is far from the case; however, it must be conceded that in the People's Republic of China, *Feng Shui* consultants are rare. Practitioners from Hong Kong, nevertheless, make regular tours of China, earning their expenses by advising on the orientation and furnishing of houses, shops and factories; and from their astrological knowledge, declaring auspicious times for weddings and funerals.

In 1986, while staying in a new hotel in Kuei-lin (the capital of the Kuang-hsi province where the Form school of *Feng Shui* originated), I was informed by the proud manager that the hotel had been carefully designed and sited in complete accordance with *Feng Shui* principles. A bend in the river in front of the hotel created a 'dragon pool' which would ensure the hotel's prosperity, although it also collected the detritus and garbage which the river brought with it. The entrance doors were sited correctly, too, but against obvious meteorological arguments, since they faced the prevailing winds from the mountains. And even though the hotel was completed, the official opening was to be delayed until the most auspicious hour on the most auspicious day.

Trying to find out more about the extent of the practice of *Feng Shui* today, I had been searching without success through the shops and bazaars of Canton, looking for a *Feng Shui* compass. Then, quite by chance, I stumbled across a tiny village general store which to my astonishment had several crudely made examples for sale. These were obviously intended for the domestic market; for though they were manufactured in Fo Shan, they grandly claimed to be from a factory called 'Hong Kong', thereby attempting to assure prospective purchasers of their authenticity.

A form of divination

In the Western world, destiny has been regarded by some as inescapable; others, as avoidable. When the Pharaoh dreamt of the seven fat and the seven lean kine, these were symbols of future events, which could be heeded, so averting the threatened famine, or ignored, and the consequences suffered. For the ancient Greeks, however, the Fates could never be thwarted.

By contrast, the influences of *Feng Shui* can be avoided, diverted, or even generated. Unlike the courses of the stars and planets, the configurations of this Earth may be changed through natural or human intervention. Thus, landscaping or earthquakes may alter the portents of *Feng Shui* in a way that the lines of the hands, or the cycles of the Heavens, can never do.

Feng Shui may be called, in the strict sense of the word, *geomancy*, which actually means divination by portents shown by the Earth. Accordingly, it is the exact complement of astrology, which is divination by signs in the Heavens. The stars and planets, being in constant motion, give notice of the changing events of the Universe, both on the Earth and outside it. The delineation of the Earth itself dictates the situation in which we find ourselves. Thus it is explained that Emperor and pauper, both born at identical moments, may have entirely different fortunes. Though the courses of their lives as revealed by the stars in the Heavens may run

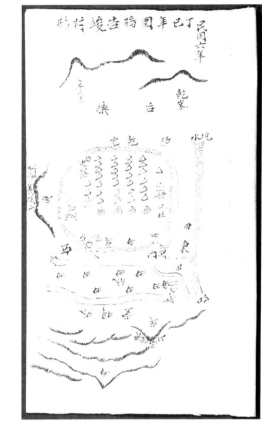

A geomancer's environmental chart for a village in China, compiled for the completion of a surrounding wall.

parallel, the differences in their circumstances are due to the serendipity of the spot where they were born.

Each individual is subject to the twin influences of the Heavens, shown by astrology, and those of the Earth, revealed by *Feng Shui*, and there are many areas where the two sciences overlap. For this reason, a geomancer will often take his client's date of birth into consideration, as this helps to identify precise directions and orientations which will be most favourable. In the case of a family home, the astrological data used will be applicable to the head of the household; while in the case of a business or institution, some significant moment – such as the date of the firm's inauguration – is taken. The astrological considerations explain, to an extent, why certain ideal *Feng Shui* locations see their fortunes rise and fall, so that there will be periods when favourable *Feng Shui* might be enhanced, but at other times neutralised, by the astrological situation. In order to establish the balance between astrological and *Feng Shui* forces, Chinese geomancers employ an instrument called the *Lo P'an* – the respected ancestor of the present mariner's compass.

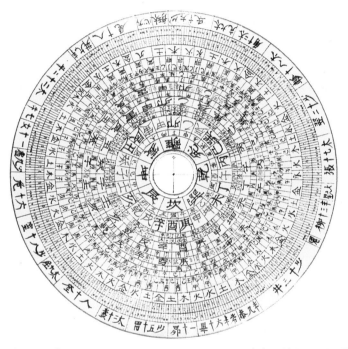

A nineteenth century Western representation of the Chinese Lo P'an, used by geomancers of the Compass school for Feng Shui calculations.

Feng Shui outside China

Although, in China itself, *Feng Shui* has always been closely linked with what are essentially religious practices, this is not necessarily the case in other parts of South-East Asia: and *Feng Shui* principles are carefully observed in communities which may be Buddhist, Muslim, or even secular. Indeed, most of the essential points of *Feng Shui* can be transferred to a Western environment without any difficulty. Town planners, architects, interior designers and landscape gardeners

can all benefit in some way from its ancient techniques. Much of its application – for example, in the emphasis laid upon the contours of the landscape – is quite simply aesthetic: and connoisseurs of Chinese art, consciously or otherwise, learn to appreciate the fine construction of landscape paintings by the same standards that determine the *Feng Shui* of an actual locality. The very same criteria also influence the design of gardens, shops, homes, and even whole cities.

Feng Shui is today practised throughout South-East Asia, wherever the Chinese have been influential. In Vietnam, ruled by China intermittently during its early history for more than a thousand years, the cities of Hue, Hanoi and Saigon were all built on a North-South alignment, in accordance with the principles of the ancient classic, The Book of Rites. Houses and villages are indeed still planned roughly in accordance with Chinese *Feng Shui* principles. For example, since North-West and West are regarded as unlucky, in setting up a home, the kitchen stove is set in the North-West to act as a barrier to evil influences.

The Vietnamese *Feng Shui* tradition seems to be mainly oral, however. The *Lo P'an* (the *Feng Shui* compass) is used, but it is a considerably simplified version of the Chinese one.

Japan has never been under Chinese rule, yet has adopted much of the Chinese culture, including a form of *Feng Shui*. A friend, living in a Western country but married to a devout Japanese lady whose father is a bonze (a Japanese priest) was obliged, at great expense, virtually to rebuild his house in accordance with *Feng Shui* principles.

More remarkable is the fact that Japanese *Feng Shui* seems to have adopted a whole pantheon of spirits who stand on guard at the sixty points of the compass. And whereas a Chinese interpretation of a particular orientation would be that the 'currents' were fortunate or harmful, the Japanese view is that the qualities inherent in a site are due to the influences of beneficial or malign spirits who take responsibility for it. The Japanese *Lo P'an* appears at first glance to be less technical than the Chinese one, but there are also certain differences in the breadth of the divisions accorded to each of the compass points, the

Chinese dividing the compass into equal parts, the Japanese according to a mathematical sequence.

The principles of *Feng Shui* are evident, too, in the great importance which the Japanese attach to proportion in their painting, their famed stone and sand gardens, their ikebana flower-arranging, and even their presentation of food. Indeed, there are few areas of Japanese thought which are not in some way affected by the influence of *Feng Shui*.

Feng Shui has also spread beyond the confines of Asia, reaching the island of Madagascar, where the tradition was introduced by early Chinese settlers: and here, too, great importance is attached to the orientation of houses, and to the display of certain talismanic emblems on the lintels of doors.

Yang and Yin sites

In China, Japan, and many other parts of the Far East, one of the most prominent features of *Feng Shui* is the role it plays in respect to disposal of the dead. Nearly all *Feng Shui* manuals enumerate long catalogues of types of terrain and their effect on *Yang* or *Yin* dwellings – the *Yang*, or positive sites, being suitable for the living, and the *Yin*, tranquil and stable sites, being appropriate for the deceased. What might be an ideal *Feng Shui* condition for a burial plot has very little to do with its lack of potential as building or agricultural land, however; in fact some lands that might be regarded as excellent locations for grave sites could be equally desirable and appropriate for residences with splendid scenic views. For it is important that ancestors should be afforded the same, or better, comforts than they had when living, so that the shades of the departed can report happily to Heaven on the piety of their children and grandchildren, and ultimately persuade the supernatural powers to bestow rewards and benefits on their descendants.

When selecting a burial site, there is no longer any necessity to take into account matters which only apply to the living – convenience for work, travel, and shopping – for instance. At the same time, some of the more abstruse requirements concerning the orientation of

A landscape painting by Dr Shinichi Suzuki, Japanese educationalist, entitled 'Man is the son of his environment'.

the monument can be observed, which might have been impossible in the construction of a Yang house.

But it is not just the selection of a site which is so important. In addition to the stationary influences of the Earth, there are the shifting cycles of Heaven to be taken into account. The very day and time of burial must therefore be concordant with the horoscope of the deceased; and in view of the scarcity of sites which have beneficial terrestial influences, it becomes incumbent to choose the day when the celestial ones will have the greatest magnaminity.

Recent years have seen *Feng Shui* playing an increasingly important role in funerals, perhaps surprisingly, now that the amount of land available for traditional burial is so limited in places such as Hong Kong and the more populated cities of the East. But if the site for burial cannot be the ideal one, its less fortunate aspects might be offset by more meticulous observance of the times for the funeral rites. Formerly, keeping the body of the deceased until the appropriate moment for the funeral, was frequently a certain health hazard. The nuisance became so serious that during the Ming Dynasty (1368–1644 AD), a law had to be passed forbidding the deceased to be kept unburied for more than a year, the penalty being eighty blows with a long stick.

Today, however, tradition and commonsense have merged. Cremation is now encouraged by many urban authorities: and not only does this enable the appropriate mourning ceremonies to be held on the most auspicious day for the deceased, it also means that the ashes can be respectfully interred in community memorial halls built in ideal *Feng Shui* locations, which would otherwise have been well beyond the means of the average family.

But it must be remembered that *Feng Shui* is not exclusively oriental. In this book, the principles of *Feng Shui* can be illustrated equally well by examples taken from one side of the world to the other. It can be seen in the distinctive network of Amsterdam's waterways, the awesome beauty of Lucerne's lacustrine seclusion; and the virtually textbook setting of Paris, with the Sacré Cœur perched pagoda-like, overlooking the ancient city.

Designing your future

But how are the theories of *Feng Shui* relevant to *your* home or place of work? And how can you adapt existing designs to beneficial effect? Whether or not a site has yet been chosen, or the first plans remain to be drawn up; or whether, in fact, a building is already finished and you, with keys in hand, are waiting to move in, the pages that follow provide suggestions as to how you can rectify any shortcomings according to *Feng Shui* principles. Ideal lay-outs are suggested; and each area, both at home and in the work-place, is considered in detail, showing you how to achieve the best *Feng Shui* with a minimum of change. Unbalanced *Feng Shui* currents may, for instance, be counteracted by a simple choice of colour on the appropriate wall, by the correct siting of a radiator or fan, or perhaps simply the careful placing of a bowl of fresh flowers. In this way, by judicious deflections of the *Feng Shui* currents, the environment at home can be made restful, and the atmosphere in the work-place more stimulating.

Finally, for an all-important section to this book, I have prepared the first Western version of the *Lo P'an* on which, for ease of reference, all the Chinese markings have been represented by recognisable figures or symbols. The Chinese *Lo P'an*, of course, has a compass needle at its centre: but an ordinary magnetic compass is now such a commonplace thing to obtain that, by following the step-by-step instructions given, there is nothing to stand in the way of the reader using this very book as a functioning *Lo P'an* instrument, in order to calculate auspicious days, favourable directions and beneficial interior arrangement.

Curiously, the Chinese formerly always constructed their maps with South at the top, and the same convention is still maintained in Chinese geomantic texts today. However, in order to assist the Western reader unfamiliar with this subject, I have opted to present all charts and diagrams in a Western form – that is, with North at the top.

The Chinese believe that whatever we do to ensure that Earth, Heaven, and Mankind are in harmony brings peace and prosperity to all. China has seen dynasties rise and fall, kingdoms absorbed into empires, and empires overthrown. But the heart of China has never ceased to beat. Bounded by the world's highest mountains, its vastest ocean, and with the only man-made construction to be visible from outer space, China has a *Feng Shui* that is eternal.

Derek Walters

PART ONE

The Landscape

*How the Perfect Location
attracts Good Fortune*

It had been quite an expedition. Old Mr Liang wanted to buy a piece of land for
his son both to live on and to farm. A neighbour, Mr Gao, happened to have
three plots for disposal; the price seemed satisfactory,
and all that remained was for a decision to be made
as to which would be the best. That morning,

Mr Liang and his son had set off early – accompanied by a few respected relatives and friends – to visit Mr Gao's estates; and by mid-day the party had finished their initial survey, a little tired after tramping the length and breadth of fields and hillsides, in order to make a thorough inspection of the available sites. But no decision had been reached as yet. For while an anxious Mrs Gao and her daughters prepared black tea and refreshments for everyone, Mr Liang and his son – aided, and bewildered, by an unrelenting stream of counsel from self-appointed advisors – discussed the advantages and liabilities of the land they had seen. Fortunately, Old Mr Liang had decided to engage the services of a famous *Feng Shui* professor. There were any number of such experts who had set up practice in the area; but the geomancer who had Mr Liang's final approval was the one remembered as being particularly knowledgeable in matters of site and scenery. Now, both parties waited anxiously for the arrival of the great authority.

喜見山多

His entrance certainly added a touch of theatricality to the proceedings. While the two farmers and their friends had been content to plod everywhere on foot, the professor arrived in a sedan chair covered, as was the custom, with a bolt of red silk, paid for, like the fees for the professor's assistants and bearers, by Old Mr Liang.

The professor first asked about Young Mr Liang's time and date of birth. It was then time to take a second tour of inspection, although now the *Feng Shui* professor's sedan and retinue imposed some formality on the proceedings. Mr Gao began to get apprehensive. Every time the sedan was set down, the sage would glance round, shake his head, and order the procession to advance. Doubtless he had his client's interests at heart, but the professor seemed to find fault with all the suggested plots. Over there, the river ran in the wrong direction; over here, winds would strike from the North-West. A particular hill had a menacing aspect; while in another location, even the gravel was too sharp.

But, just when the two farmers were beginning to despair of ever closing the contract, the professor gave a shout and ordered the procession to halt. In great excitement, he threw himself out of the sedan and pointed to a hill which had a stream and a few cultivated fields in front of it. "Look!" he cried. "A Dragon, salivating gold and silver! Let Young Mr Liang make his home here, and he and his descendants will certainly be prosperous."

The signs of relief quickly gave way to a chorus of congratulations. Though no-one else but the *Feng Shui* professor, and possibly his assistant, had the remotest perception of the Dragon salivating gold and silver, the important thing was that Mr Gao could now close his sale with Old Mr Liang, and Young Mr Liang could look forward to forging a new life for himself and his family.

Incidents such as this would have been repeated dozens, if not hundreds of times a week during pre-revolutionary times: and, *Feng Shui* experts are still in demand. Today, however, in place of the bolt of silk, the client presents the consultant with payment in cash, in a discreet red envelope. Although no fee is actually discussed, it reflects the wealth of the client and the value of the undertaking. (For example, in 1987, an afternoon's visit to a site on behalf of a client in the middle-income bracket was rewarded with one thousand Hong Kong dollars.)

The *Feng Shui* professor employed by Old Mr Liang was a master of the Form school of *Feng Shui*, in which greater emphasis was placed on the importance of the shapes and contours of the landscape and skyline, whether natural or man-made. Though the professor, like many professionals, may have clothed his report with high-sounding phrases and mystical terms, the essentials of 'shape' or Form *Feng Shui* are really quite straightforward.

Wind and Water

The term *Feng Shui*, literally translated, means 'Wind and Water'; and these are regarded as being akin to certain forces, called *ch'i* (meaning breath, air, or current), through which *Feng Shui* operates.

In ancient times, the wind was regarded as the divine breath, and great attention was given to the direction in which it blew, since any unseasonal direction was regarded as a portent from Heaven. A Southerly wind was usually a welcome sign, since South and South-Westerly winds brought warmth to the North of China, and the vital rains to the South. By contrast, North and North-Easterly winds brought both freezing cold and drought, so winds from these directions were regarded as bad omens.

When all was right with the world – or, as the philosophers would say, Heaven and Earth were in harmony – the winds would blow at their appropriate seasons: the North winds in winter, the South winds in summer. But if Heaven had been offended, then the country would be visited by searing famine, torrential floods, or ravaging typhoons. The great Chinese classic, the *Shi-chi*, or 'Records of the Historian', written in the second century BC, makes it clear that: '*When the winds blow harmoniously and the rains come down regularly, the Realm shall flourish.*'

So it was that the sages of old decreed that the best site for a city was one screened from the inauspicious Northerly winds by a protective barrier of mountains or hills. In later centuries, when the study of *Feng Shui* came to be more precise and systemized, the original purpose of selecting mountains for a background – as a guard against the winds – came to be forgotten. Instead, the qualities which were regarded as crucial to the *Feng Shui* of an area came to depend not so much on the *size* of any mountains or hills, but their actual *shapes*.

The second word in the expression '*Feng Shui*' means water. This is essential for any community, not just for drinking, but to enable a civilisation to function: and all cities of the Old World had to be built near water, on the shores of seas, lakes or rivers, principally because water meant transport, transport brought commerce, and commerce generated wealth.

But a family looking for somewhere to settle would have to take other considerations into account, too. Upstream, where the water was less polluted, the population would be less liable to disease: while downstream, where the land flattened and fanned out, there would be a greater likelihood of flooding, with all the resultant damage and danger. Perhaps instinctively, or perhaps quite consciously, the early exponents of *Feng Shui* would have taken these sensible guidelines as the foundation for their theories.

However, just as the original significance of 'wind' in 'Wind and Water' has been lost, the same is true, but to a lesser extent, of 'water'. It remains important to search out springs, observe water flow, and the courses of streams, to find the *Feng Shui* of the landscape, but it no longer matters if the beds of the streams, rivers, and ponds are actually dry. This is because it is not the water itself which is thought to be the carrier of the vital *ch'i*, but rather the line traced by the continuously descending paths of the streams.

As, however, there is very little that the ordinary person can do to alter the shape of the landscape, perhaps the wisest course of action for anyone moving to a new area is to follow the example of old Mr Liang in the story on pages 16-18, and ensure that the *Feng Shui* of the region is right from the start.

Dragons and Tigers

Find the Dragon, and you have the key to a site's *Feng Shui*. It might appear in the contours of the surrounding hills, when it is known as a 'true Dragon'; or perhaps in the silhouette of a man-made skyline; or even, if the area is unremittingly flat and plain, in the shapes of fields or patterns created by streams and pathways, when it is known as a 'false Dragon', and not quite so favourable.

One hill rising above the others and to the East, North-East or South-East of a site is regarded as a 'true' Dragon.

The true Dragon is seen in a hill rising above the others, one slope rising sharply, the other falling away, and to the East, North-East or South-East of a site. An imaginative eye, cast over the shape and contour of the hill, will be able to discern features which can be identified as parts of the Dragon's anatomy: knolls along the ridge will be identified as the Dragon's backbone, for instance; elsewhere, a stream might be salivations from its open mouth. Kuo Hsi, a famous Sung Dynasty landscape painter of the eleventh century, said that: "*Watercourses are the arteries of a mountain, grass and trees its hair; mist and haze it's complexion*": and his students would have understood the description to apply to the 'Dragon' of the mountain.

It is widely known that the name of Hong Kong's mainland district, Kowloon, means 'Nine Dragons', eight of the dragons being the hills on which Kowloon stands, and the ninth being the Emperor. When speaking of scenery, the words 'mountain' and 'Dragon' are virtually synonymous: and even in modern, post-revolutionary China, mountains are still spoken of as if they were living organisms. Professor Chen Cong Zhou of Tongji University, Shanghai, for example, in a paper urging conservation of the environment published in the University's Journal in 1980, complained that inconsiderate construction work and urban development were causing mountain springs – "the eyes of the mountains" – to dry up and become lost forever.

The true Dragon will also be complemented by another geographical feature, this time to the West of the site and known as the Tiger. In fact, *Feng Shui* manuals state quite clearly that where is a true Dragon, there must also be a Tiger, as if the two were inseparable, like the head and tail of a coin. When there is only one hill to be considered, then the Dragon will be the higher point, merging into the lower, gentler slopes of the Tiger. More usually, however, the Dragon and Tiger are perceived as two distinguishable hills. Ideally, these will form a pair of hills meeting in a horse-shoe or bow shape. If one ridge folds behind the other, like two clasped hands, this is regarded as the best shape of all, and is said to represent the Dragon a Tiger in embrace.

Here, the Dragon and Tiger are in embrace, which is said to be the most favourable aspect of all.

The area in front of the bow – the site protected by the *Feng Shui* of the Dragon and Tiger – should be open, and facing South, so that the two mountains form a barrier against the cold North winds. In this way, the Dragon is to be found Eastwards of a site, and the Tiger, Westwards. Because of this, a favourably-shaped hill, with

all the evidence of the bones, limbs, hair and arteries, which painters are urged to seek, is considered a Dragon if viewed from one vantage point, but a Tiger if seen from another.

The Four Directions

The terms Dragon and Tiger are taken from Chinese astronomy, which divides the Heavens into four great constellations: the Green Dragon of the East, the Red Bird of the South, the White Tiger of the West, and the Black Tortoise of the North.

In an ideal site, the Southern aspect is left open to the sun, and so there is no 'Bird' mountain shape at this point; while if the Dragon and Tiger 'embrace', they shut out the malevolent winds of the Northern Tortoise.

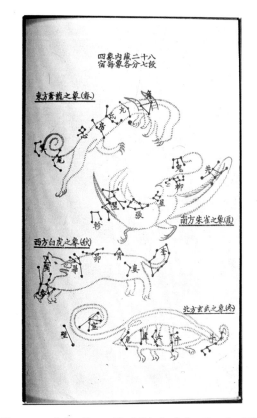

The Green Dragon of the East, Red Bird of the South, White Tiger of the West, and Black Tortoise of the North.

The Pagoda

The statuesque and distinctive many-terraced Chinese pagoda has an ancient and somewhat curious history. It was as a dome-shaped Indian memorial burial mound called a *stupa* that, with the rise of Buddhism, the pagoda began a significant part of its evolution into the typically Chinese form known today. In the third century BC the *stupa*, now an important Buddhist shrine, arrived in China where its structure was to merge over the centuries with indigenous Chinese architecture. By the sixth century AD, Indian and Chinese architectural influences on the shrine had become synthesized into a taller, more abstract form; and balconies – no longer functional – became integrated simply as a design feature. Eventually, the pagoda lost its original religious significance, becoming instead an entirely secular landmark. However, it continued to find a role in society, both as a venue for popular festivities, and a place of protection. Always possessing an odd number of storeys, usually seven or nine, it was, at times, frequently built in order to create propitious *Feng Shui*. Pagodas are found throughout China – a testimony, perhaps, to their continuing contribution both to the beauty of the landscape and to the well-being of the people.

But in order to emphasize the continuing harmony between the Heavens and Earth, ideally it should be possible also to identify some aspects of the scenery to the South and North that represent the other two constellations. A boulder or some other feature of the South might, with imagination, be seen as a perched bird, for example; while to the North, a stretch of water could be the emblem of the Tortoise. It is not necessary for these landmarks to be natural aspects of the landscape: even artificial additions to the scene – buildings or bridges, for instance – are regarded as part of the essential shape of the surrounding area. (Interestingly, the original purpose of such identifying landmarks is likely to have been for astronomical study since, before the invention of clocks, the time of night could only be reckoned by the position of the stars at fixed points on the skyline, an ancient tradition which *Feng Shui* has preserved to this day.)

Although a site cannot be considered to be completely in tune with all the *Feng Shui* influences unless each of the four quarters of the Heavens – Dragon, Bird, Tiger and Tortoise – can be readily identified, for most purposes it is sufficiently auspicious to be able to identify the Dragon and the Tiger. The Dragon, being the first of the constellations and identified with spring, growth, creation, and the life-giving rains, takes precedence over the Tiger, more properly associated with autumn and harvests. But just as there cannot be an East without a West, so the presence of the Dragon implies the existence of the Tiger, and consequently it is enough to be able to point out the Dragon to the East of the site. However, if the East of the site is flat, without the least sign of a Dragon hill, then – as a last resort – the presence of a Tiger (a suitable rise to the West of the site) will save the situation and render the spot a reasonably favourable one.

Water Dragons

A true Dragon is one found in an undulating landscape. Some *Feng Shui* scholars maintain that flat-lying land is lifeless, lacking *ch'i*: that is, the breath or essential currents produced by the folds of hills. In his *Water Dragon Classic*, now regarded as the standard text on the subject, Chiang Ping-chieh, a Ming Dynasty philosopher, states that *ch'i* can also be found in the patterns made by water-courses on fairly level ground. Just as the Dragons and Tigers of mountains generate terrestial *ch'i*, so the flow of water is said to generate its own brand of aquatic *ch'i*. Rivers, canals, streams and their tributaries are thus all regarded as manifestations of the Water Dragon. And in practice, the more level the ground, the more sinuous and branched is the flow of water in the region, while the greater the number of these confluences, the more powerful the *ch'i*.

Since the *Water Dragon Classic*, shelves of books on water formations have been written, with long complex catalogues of every likely – and unlikely – combination of water-courses, canal and dock systems. But basically, all the various combinations are derived from a few simple principles founded on observation and logic.

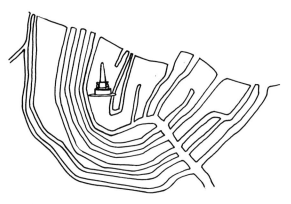

This network of semi-circular canals forms a favourable Water-Dragon.

The mouth of a valley or a fan-shaped delta, for instance, is usually regarded as being a very inauspicious area, not illogical since it is liable to flooding. But if a network of branches and tributaries, instead of dispersing into the sea, first partly encloses a site, this is regarded as extremely favourable, bringing wealth and profit to the region. Favourable sites such as these are said to be Water Dragons, and are illustrated in *Feng Shui* manuals with diagrams which look remarkably like the unmistakeable network of semi-circular canals found in the city of Amsterdam, Holland.

Feng Shui experts also advise that it is important not to be situated too close to the mainstream, where the *ch'i* flows too quickly to provide any beneficial influence, while a mainstream with no tributaries is regarded as potentially barren.

Fast-flowing, straight rivers, and water which flows directly North to South bring no advantage; but streams flowing East to West (in either direction) are regarded as favourable, linking – as they do – the directions associated with the Dragon and the Tiger.

Water flowing to the front of a building promises good Feng Shui.

Water to the South of a site, flowing calmly, is regarded as very favourable, as it brings wealth. Gentle meanders allow riches to accumulate, but sharp bends, are reminiscent of arrows, and considered a danger. Anywhere directly facing a current, but particularly when the current flows from the North, is also considered to be in an unfavourable position: and certainly, such places are more liable to be subject to both erosion and flooding.

London's Thames is a good example of a river which has a favourable flow. Its overall direction is East-West, rather than North-South; it flows slowly, meandering rather than flowing straight; and it has numerous tributaries. Some locations on the Thames – for example, those situated in South-facing loops – will be more favourable than others; while some, because they face a sharp current from the North, may be at a distinct disadvantage from a *Feng Shui* point-of-view. But the overall aspect of the Thames is destined to bring prosperity.

London's Thames has a generally favourable flow.

Watercourses which divide and branch off are regarded as unfavourable, since the *ch'i* is similarly divided and dissipated. Conversely, a site where two streams flow parallel and then into each other is highly favourable, involving the concentration of two currents of *ch'i*. However, if the streams meet in collision, though it may result in a spectacular display of water sculpture, this is regarded as harmful to the *Feng Shui* of the area, since the *ch'i* of the two streams is mutually broken.

The rapid growth of urban and industrial development in Hong Kong today means that modern experts in mountain and water *Feng Shui* are just as busy as their great-grandfathers were a century ago. But the difference is that, while their ancestors would have been consulted about the location of a single farmhouse, today's needs are for advice concerning the vast housing complexes and industrial sites which are biting into the sides of the mountains.

But whether for entire cities or simple cottages, the same *Feng Shui* principles hold good: and the private individual who is fortunate enough to have few restrictions on the choice of a site for a new home or even an established property will have nothing to lose by weighing the available options according to the quality of the area's *Feng Shui*.

PART TWO

The Site

How the Perfect Orientation stimulates Success

Lin had a thriving hardware business in town. Its success owed much to the fact that Lin and his wife could always be relied upon to be available at all hours of the day and night. But the time had come when they felt sufficiently secure to be able to afford to live away from the shop, although they did not want to move to such a distance that a messenger could not reach them within a few minutes. So when a plot of land became available opposite the neighbourhood temple, it seemed like a gift from Heaven. Mr Wang, a wealthy merchant, and the owner of the land, had taken great pains to

Tortoise to the North. But in towns, more often than not, a South-facing building is impracticable: streets have houses on both sides, and if all houses faced South, half of them would have their backs to the road. Fortunately, this is a problem that can be resolved realistically.

Every house is seen as its own little universe. For this reason, *Feng Shui* speaks of the four sides of the house in the same terms as those used for the four compass directions. The front, which ideally should face South, is called the Red Bird, whatever the direction it faces, while the back is referred to as the Black Tortoise. Similarly, with the back to the Tortoise, the left side is the Green Dragon; and the right, the White Tiger. The authoritative source on *Feng Shui* for House Construction, the *Yang-chai Ching*, (The Classic of Dwellings) maintains that: "*All residences are honourable which have on the left flowing water, representing the Green Dragon; on the right a long path, symbolising the White Tiger; in the front a pool, for the Red Bird; and at the back a hill, the emblem of the Black Tortoise.*"

Thus, although any town house on the 'wrong' side of the street may be facing the reverse direction to tradition, it is still possible to avoid any adverse effects if the environment is seen to be in accordance with the Four Directions. In any case, this means that the back and sides of the site should be enclosed, and just the front open. Closing the sides ensures that beneficial *ch'i* do not disperse into the surrounding area.

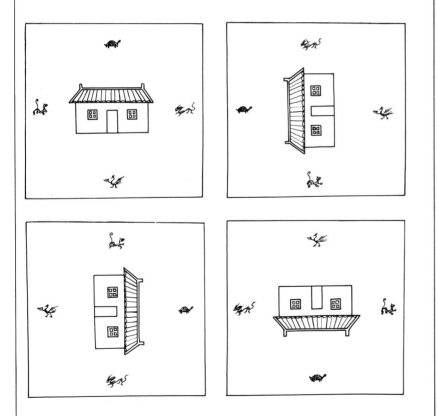

The front of the house, whichever direction it faces, is known as the Red Bird; the back, the Black Tortoise; the left side, facing outwards from the front, the Green Dragon; and the right, the White Tiger.

Evergreen influences

Obstacles in front of the house are regarded as extremely bad omens. For example, a boulder or mound blocking a direct path up to the house entrance is said to result in family troubles, and would therefore have to be physically removed. Similarly, large trees in front of

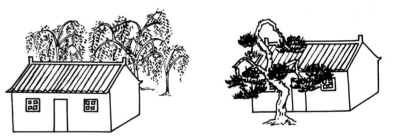

Trees to the back of a house are said to be favourable, particularly if evergreen: but large trees to the front are inauspicious.

a house are said to indicate family separation. However, trees to the Black Tortoise side are regarded as auspicious, since they protect the house from unfavourable winds. Preferably, too, these trees should have plenty of foliage, and the more luxuriant they are, the better the prosperity of the family, while evergreens are best of all. Care of trees is seen as vital, and it is important not to scar or damage *Feng Shui* trees in any way, lest this affect the welfare of the residents under their protective influence. In China, many temples also have *Feng Shui* trees which are considered almost sacred. In Northern China, these are usually pine trees (a symbol of virtue and longevity); and in the South, banyan, associated with the Buddha.

Secret arrows

It is not uncommon for the view from a house to be worth more than its bricks and mortar. But sadly, it often happens that the landscape which was so dearly bought becomes ravaged by some ugly development, and there is little or no recompense for those who have to suffer it most. In China, private individuals formerly had recourse to the magistrate if it could be shown that their *Feng Shui* was in danger of being destroyed: and before work could be started on any project, advance notice would have to be posted up so that the neighbours could lodge their objections if they felt endangered.

Even today, when investigating the *Feng Shui* of a site, any possible *sha*, or evil influences, have to be identified: for just as streams or other watercourses pointing at a site are believed to be carriers of fatal currents (dry river beds have an untimely tendency to become raging torrents), so

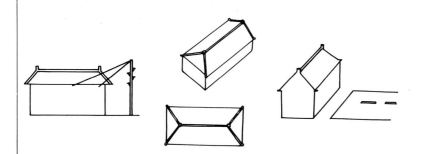

The inauspicious influences of sha may originate from such features as telegraph poles, pointed roofs or roadways.

it is deemed important that a building does not stand in the path of any direct straight lines, as these are possible conveyors of *sha*, too.

Consistent with the rough generalisation that there are no straight lines in nature, *sha* are usually of artificial origin, and take the form of canals, roads, streets and paths, railway lines, the ridges of roofs and the edges of buildings, or even telegraph wires. Rarely, they can also be seen in the landscape in the form of geological faults.

Even more ominous than the straight line is the 'secret arrow' or hidden pointer created by a sharp bend or angle in a river, road, or the fabric of a building: and under no circumstances should this be seen to point to

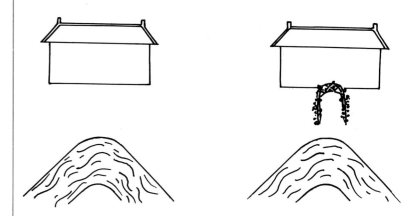

A simple rose trellis, or some other ornamental feature, may suffice to deflect the unfavourable sha of a watercourse pointing at the house.

a door or window in the house, as its existence poses a certain threat to the well-being of the residents there.

Fortunately, such unfavourable influences can be remedied: and if it is impossible to avoid the presence of *sha* or 'secret arrows', they can be blocked or deflected in a number of ways, according to their nature. Distant *sha*, especially those formed by geological formations, walls and embankments, can be deflected by trees. Sharper, more precisely directed 'secret arrows', such as those formed by the corner of a building, could be blocked by a suitably sited wall or an ornamental feature standing between the source and the house: while, if there is no obvious need for a free-standing wall, or even one which might function as the side of a shed or porch, some other feature – such as a rose trellis, might be considered.

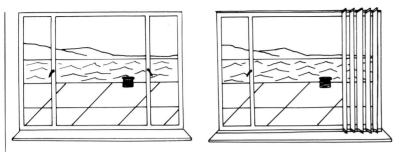

Windows should not open on to the downstream of a river, but blinds may remedy such poor Feng Shui. The same principle applies to main drainage, too: although since water-mains usually run underground, this need not cause undue concern.

Watercourses

Today's *Feng Shui* consultant will also examine the position and direction of the water-mains and drainage, since these have the same function as the streams and watercourses of earlier times.

Good *Feng Shui* occurs when water flows down to the rear of the building, not directly, but to its right or left side, passing in front of the site, and leaving in a direction at right-angles to the direction in which it arrived. In other words, the foundations ought to be made in the crook of a right angle, the front facing the same direction as the arriving flow. It is acceptable for bends in any water-course, whether natural or mains water, to point away from the house; but bends pointing towards the house need to be avoided, as these constitute 'secret arrows', again foreboding potential danger to the family.

One unusual maxim is that once water has passed by the site, it should no longer be visible, as it is otherwise believed to carry off essential *ch'i*. In practical terms, this means that windows should not open on to the downstream of a river. Fortunately, this is not something which need always concern town dwellers unduly, as water-mains usually run underground. (Most *Feng Shui* precepts usually have a sound underlying reason; and in this case it is probably because water flowing away from the site would usually mean the drains, which ought to be covered for sanitary reasons.)

The Five Elements

At the heart of any of the Chinese sciences and related disciplines – medicine, acupuncture, music, fine art, and even cuisine – lies the unshakeable principle of the Five Elements: Wood, Fire, Earth, Metal and Water. These are considered to stimulate and shape all natural and human activity.

The Wood Element symbolizes all life, femininity, creativity, and organic material; Fire is the Element of energy and intelligence; Earth, the Element of stability, endurance and the earth itself; Metal, in addition to its material sense, also encompasses competitiveness, business acumen, and masculinity; while Water is the Element of all that flows – oil and alcohol as well as water itself, consequently also symbolizing transport and communication.

When considering the *Feng Shui* of the landscape, the essential features associated with the Five Elements must be taken into account. Tall, cylindrical features, which can be thought of as trunks of trees, belong to the Element Wood; sharp peaks (like darting flames) to the Element Fire; flat, eroded terrain, to the Element Earth; rounded hills (think of them as coins), to Metal; and wavy, undulating ground, to Water.

Identifying the Elements in the skyline round a particular site also makes it possible to evaluate any likely dangers. Thus houses based at the foot of a Metal-shape hill are said to be more liable to theft and burglary (possibly because the rounded hill makes it easier for the criminal to make an attack and quick get-away). Forewarned, those living in such locations are advised to pay greater attention to security measures and to take out adequate insurance.

Unlike the elements of Western science, the Five Elements are regarded as being interactive, each Element capable of generating another in a *productive* order. Thus, burning Wood produces Fire; Fire leaves behind Earth; Earth is the source of Metal; Metal can be liquified into substances flowing like Water; while Water helps live Wood to thrive. The *productive* Element is always beneficial, generating and stimulating the Element succeeding it.

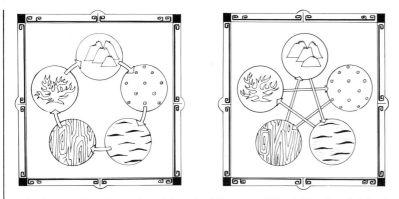

*Left The **productive** order of the Five Elements: Wood-Fire-Earth-Metal-Water. Right The **destructive** order: Wood-Earth-Water-Fire-Metal.*

But there is also a *destructive* order, Wood-Earth-Water-Fire-Metal, which is considered harmful. (Wood takes nourishment from the Earth; Earth muddies Water; Water quenches Fire; and Fire melts Metal.) It is considered weak or even harmful if two Elements next to each other in the destructive sequence are in close proximity. For example, crops – represented by the Element Wood – might be in constant danger of being plundered if there were rounded hills nearby, as these represent the Element Metal, the Element of swords and ploughshares.

To avoid such harmful effects, a *controlling* Element should be present, this Element being the one which generates the Element under threat in the *productive* order. In the example above, if a stream ran between the crops and the hill, the danger would be averted, Water being the controlling Element.

A matter of shape

Unless some peculiarity of the site dictated a particular ground plan, Chinese houses always adhered to a traditional design, followed for centuries. In recent years, however, as architecture has become more adventurous, the novel forms have raised some intriguing *Feng Shui* problems – usually for the neighbouring residents.

The ideal site is rectangular, the four sides aligned with the four compass points: and if the length and breadth are each divided into three, so forming nine plots, the building itself should occupy the middle one, since this is considered the most harmonious use of proportions and ground space. But in densely populated areas, and in locations crossed by roads, watercourses, or hillsides, the shape of the available site may be dictated by

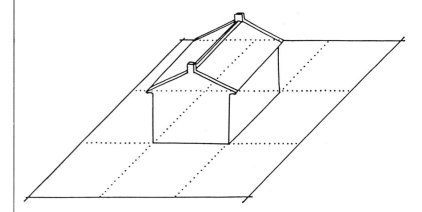

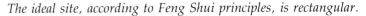

The ideal site, according to Feng Shui principles, is rectangular.

geographical conditions, and unfavourable *Feng Shui* will have to be remedied.

Triangular plots are anathema. The shape represents Fire; and to avoid the threat of conflagration, geomancers advise that one side of the triangle be cut off by running a wall or hedge parallel to one of the sides to produce a trapezium-shaped plot. The remaining smaller triangle should be similarly disguised with a boundary line parallel

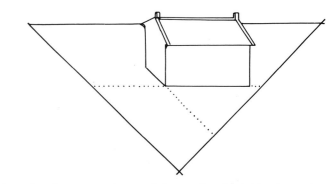

Triangular plots are not favoured, but can be adapted to a trapezium shape.

to another side, and the other piece used to create an ornamental feature, such as a small garden.

By the same token, square plots are regarded as ideal because the square is the symbol of the Element Earth, and so suggests stability and endurance. Long narrow strips of land – not entirely practical and appropriate to the Element Wood – are unfavourable from a *Feng Shui* point of view since Wood draws strength from the Earth. The inference is that the fabric of the building might be weakened in time. However, if the strip were used for a row of terraced units (shops or houses), then each plot would tend more towards the favoured rectangular shape. Irregular shaped plots belong to the Element Water, and would be best suited to a tall, narrow structure representing the Element Wood, since Water feeds Wood. The circle represents both the Element Metal and Heaven, as opposed to the (planet) Earth, so that the

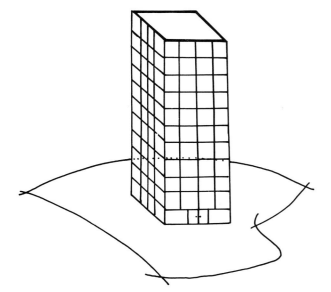

Irregular plots are best suited to tall, narrow buildings.

circular shape is probably more suited to finance houses or religious buildings.

A house built with a narrow frontage, but widening to the back is regarded as extremely favourable, since it signifies increasing prosperity and many descendants. It is crucial, however, to ensure that the rear of the building

is adequately secured and protected to safeguard such prosperity. Irregularly shaped plots ought also to be avoided if they dictate that the building should have acute-angled corners, since these are considered to harbour stagnant areas of malarial *sha*, bringing the threat of disease. (It could be that the origin of this precept lies in the fact that awkward angles, difficult to reach and clean, may harbour all kinds of pests and unpleasantness.)

L-shaped plots pose problems of another kind, since they are visualised as rectangles lacking one corner, and possibly representing the absence of the head of the household, long-life, or prosperity. It will not matter so much, however, if the missing corner is at an 'unlucky' direction, for example, the North. This would be an occasion when the *Feng Shui* professor would carefully examine the site with the *Lo P'an*, in order to advise on the best location of particular rooms within the building.

Stable foundations

The stability of a building depends on having good foundations. Consequently, the careful geomancer will examine the soil or gravel to evaluate its Element type. Formerly, every house would need to have its own kitchen garden for a ready supply of vegetables, so the soil would have to be assessed on its horticultural merits, as well as its suitability as a house foundation.

The ancient compilers of *Feng Shui* manuals seem to have been familiar with surveying techniques, and were aware, for example, of the need for effective damp coursing, even though their explanations were framed in the mystical language of their science. Ground *ch'i*, they stated, must flow gently, and the earth must be permitted to breathe. Hollows which do not allow the ground to respire, and hard, rocky soil are lifeless: but red loamy soil, the colour of Fire, is full of life.

The *Yang-chai Ching* (The Classic of Dwellings) also warns against building over stumps of trees and disused wells, explaining the dangers in philosophical language. The wood draws vital *ch'i* from the house, and wells store noxious *sha*. A modern-day surveyor might add that tree roots thought dead may yet be growing, possibly causing the foundations to be disturbed; while apart from the obvious hazards of having an open shaft beneath a house, disused wells might indeed be sources of damp, marsh gas, or disease.

Other locations which the *Yang-chai Ching* advises against are the mouths of thoroughfares, which at one time were, of course, subject to the noise and wear of passing carriages, just as modern streets are affected by heavy vehicles. For similar reasons, locations near town gates are to be avoided: and sites near shrines, temples and churches, even though they might appear to be spiritually reassuring, are thought to be a source of a variety of unwelcome nuisances of human, if not supernatural, origin.

Roofs and elevation

Buildings, whether of modern or traditional design, can be classified according to the Five Elements, following the same general principles that apply to the contours of the landscape. Thus, sharply pointed roofs belong to the Fire Element; low, flat roofs to the Earth Element; domes, to Metal; irregular shapes to Water, and tall, narrow constructions to the Wood Element. The significance of the Element type is of further importance when relating the building to its environment. A Fire-type building, for example, would be unlikely to prosper in a neighbourhood where the predominant Element is Water, since Water quenches Fire.

Similarly, it would be unwise for an enterprise to commission an irregularly shaped building (representing Water) in an area where most of the buildings had flat (Earth-shape) roofs, since Water is sullied by Earth, suggesting that competition from neighbouring concerns would prevent the business from succeeding. The converse applies to any enterprise housed in a squat flat-roofed building surrounded by a forest of high-rise office blocks since, just as trees draw their strength from the soil, Wood conquers Earth.

The number of storeys to a building has never been of serious concern to the Chinese geomancer, and there are several reasons for this. Apart from the many-storeyed

Pointed roofs belong to the Element Fire; domes to Metal; tall, narrow buildings to Wood; low, flat roofs to Earth; and irregular shapes to Water.

pagodas, which had an external rather than internal function, the emphasis in Chinese architecture is towards the effective use of horizontal rather than vertical space, a perception seen at its most dramatic in the expansive vistas of the Forbidden City in Peking.

On a more mundane level, it was considered distasteful for commoners to live in high buildings, which would enable them to gaze idly into the private enclaves of their superiors: and there was even a law forbidding people below a certain rank, whatever their wealth, to have a house of more than two storeys. Consequently, there is no traditional canon of guidance concerning the merits of particular floors in high-rise buildings or offices. This is one of the very few areas in which the ancient *Feng Shui* traditions do not apply to modern day living. For streams and water-courses, there are water-mains; for the preservation of beneficial Dragons, we have the conservation of the landscape; while the dangers of the secret arrows are only too evident to someone living by an angle in a main road. The texts and precepts may be ancient, but they still apply in general to a modern age.

The Ming T'ang

The pool of water which Yang Yün-sung (founder of the Form school of *Feng Shui*) declared should be placed in front of the house, is one of the dominant themes of *Feng Shui*. The pool is known as the *Ming T'ang*, a name taken from the Ancient Book of Rites and meaning 'Bright Hall', originally a hall in the Emperor's palace used for religious ceremonials. The expression was adopted by Chinese astrologers as a technical term, and from there it found its way into *Feng Shui* theory. The importance of the *Ming T'ang* probably derives from the fact that the Southern prospect of any site was expected to be unobstructed. Since water is flat, a pond in the South would ensure a minimum of unobstructed space in front of the house.

The ideal shape for the *Ming T'ang* is a semi-circle, with the straight edge on the house side, and the curve bowed out away from the house. Irregular-shaped pools are not favoured, the *Yang-chai Ching* (*The Classic of Dwellings for the Living*) stating that children born in a house with a 'broken' *Ming T'ang* will not attain an official position, but remain as labourers. Nor are circular ponds approved since, according to the same authority, they are thought to harbour disease.

Though the *Ming T'ang* is almost an obligatory recommendation for houses with deficient *Feng Shui*, its form and nature have always varied very considerably. Some were functional reservoirs; others, ornamental ponds; still others, sunken gardens: while in the case of temples and larger, formal residences which would have been built according to the most ideal *Feng Shui* principles, the *Ming T'ang* reverted to its original purpose as a ceremonial area, and would be either a hall or courtyard. As these were customarily painted in red (the colour of the South and the Fire Element), the term 'vermilion courtyard' was occasionally used in flowery language to mean ponds and tanks constructed for *Feng Shui* purposes.

The *Ming T'ang* is particularly recommended when there is no natural water flowing by the house. This usage obviously stems from the days before piped water supplies existed, when rain would be the only source of water. As it ran down the roofs and over the sloping sides of the tanks, the rain was considered to collect beneficial *ch'i*. Even today, it is not uncommon to see people collecting rain water dripping from the roofs of temples, for medicinal purposes, as it is thought to hold the most efficacious *ch'i* of all.

But in cases where the *Ming T'ang* was no more than a depression or sunken garden in front of the house, its prime purpose was not so much to act as a store-house of *ch'i*, but rather to ensure that the view in front of the building was kept unobstructed.

PART THREE

The Home

*How the Perfect Arrangement
creates Contentment*

Widow Mao grudgingly poured a cupful of rice into the monk's begging
bowl. He took the offering humbly. It saddened him to take a gift from
an old woman who was so poor herself, but sacrifice was a virtuous
act, and it would bring her merit in Heaven.

"Don't forget you promised me a charm to help my
back; it's no better."

He rummaged in his scrip, and handed her
a talisman, printed on yellow paper. She stared
at it doubtfully. "And is this going to rid the
house of all the evil spirits that plague it?"
The monk looked puzzled.

智法避邪

"It isn't just my health," she sighed. "This is an unlucky house. You know about these things. Can't you improve this apartment, too?"

"How is it unlucky?" he asked.

"Things disappear all the time. They just vanish."

"You mean you lose them, or they are stolen?"

"No, no. At first I thought that thieves were robbing me. Then Chang's boy offered to fit a new lock for five yuan. That was robbery, if anything was. I had the lock fixed, yet things still disappear."

"What sort of things?"

"Anything. My brooch. The ring my aunt gave me. Money, sometimes."

"You haven't mislaid them, perhaps?"

"They've gone, I tell you."

The monk was perplexed. This was such an unlikely place for evil spirits and supernatural agencies to be at work. Yet the apartment did seem to have a certain malignant atmosphere, dark and unwelcoming, as it most definitely was.

"The stairs lead right up to your door. That isn't good for the *Feng Shui*. And the door opens the wrong way. Could you have it turned round?"

"And who will do that? I paid five yuan to have the lock fixed. Five yuan! I could live for a week on that."

The monk pondered. "I will make you a special talisman which will be. . ."

"As effective as the charms for my rheumatism, I expect."

"No, this will be a very powerful charm: a magic demon-dispelling mirror, with the Eight Symbols written on it. It will deflect all the evil influences which are affecting this house."

Widow Mao thought for a moment, then shook her head vigorously. "No, no. A good idea, perhaps, but where am I going to get the money to pay for such a thing as this?"

"The Buddha will provide it" said the monk, quietly.

Some days later, the monk called again with a present for the Widow Mao. It was a little convex mirror, held in a red frame on which the Eight Trigrams had been painted in gold. It was, he assured the widow, the most powerful talisman of all. No demons could withstand it.

The evil spirits responsible for carrying off the widow's possessions would surely be exposed and put to flight.

Her gratitude mingled with doubt, the old widow let the monk fix the mirror to the wall opposite the entrance door. Her simple philosophy, born of years of experience, was to wait and see.

It was a few days after the monk's visit that the efficacy of the magic mirror was to prove its worth, but in a way that was entirely unexpected.

Widow Mao had been sitting in the kitchen, pounding beans for a sauce, when she became aware of a strange flicker in the light, as if a bird had flown across the room. But there was no bird: only a quiet, ominous creak. She looked up, and from her chair saw the magic mirror darken, then brighten again.

Very slowly, and silently, she put down the dish, and crossed the room. To her surprise, she saw that the door, which ought to have been firmly locked, was now slightly ajar. She looked again at the mirror; and, through its distorted reflection, could see on one side into her tiny kitchen, and on the other, into her bedroom. What she saw there told her everything.

With great effort, and not making a sound, she knelt down. Carefully, she took her walking stick and held it steady. She only had to wait a minute before Chang's boy, the very boy who had charged her five yuan for fitting her lock, emerged from the bedroom. As he crept past, she lunged out with her stick, hooked him by the ankle and sent him careering down the stairs.

The next time the monk came to see her, Widow Mao was a changed person. In great merriment, she told him what had happened, and how Chang, mortified and humiliated by the incident, had managed to recover some of her little treasures from his wayward son.

"Pass me your bowl, old teacher," she laughed.

"Here's the five yuan I paid for the lock. Give it to someone who needs it more than I do now."

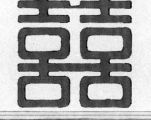

House Numbers

In the Western hemisphere, the figure 7 is often considered to be lucky, and 13 to be unlucky. The Chinese, on the other hand, attach no particular significance to the number 7, while 13 – of Buddhist religious significance and also the number of lunar months in the year – is regarded as being extremely fortunate.

But certain numbers appear to be luckier when written in the Western style. For example, the figure 88 looks like the Chinese character for 'Double Happiness' – a most auspicious door number for a young married couple. Eight is also the number of the immortals, the trigrams of the *I Ching*, and the number of characters in a Chinese date of birth.

When the Chinese character for 'long life' is written in flowing script, the lower part of the character resembles the Western figure 9. Consequently, if a Chinese house number contains a 9, the owner would be sure to have it posted in Western rather than Chinese numerals. Nine is also the number of mansions in the *Book of Rites*, and the number of Lights of Heaven – the Sun, Moon, and Seven Stars (of the Great Bear).

Other preferred digits are 5, the number of the Chinese Elements; and 6, which is said to bring wealth. Oddly enough, the figure 1 is not particularly liked, perhaps because the Chinese character resembles the bar to a door, and would hardly be appropriate for an entrance. The only number which is actually disliked is the figure 4, which Chinese gamblers say brings bad luck.

Among higher numbers which are regarded as fortunate are 24, the number of divisions in the Chinese solar calendar; 28, which is the number of constellations in the Chinese lunar calendar; 64 (8 × 8), the number of diagrams in the *I Ching*; and 81 (9 × 9), the chapters of the *Tao Te Ching* (*The Way of Virtue*, the classic of Taoism); and 100.

The Entrance

Once a site has been chosen, the prospective house-builder may employ a geomancer to consult with the architect in order to ensure the best possible arrangement of the rooms.

The positioning of the entrance is of prime concern, as this dictates the orientation of the whole house.

The entrance is the public face of a building. It gives visitors and passers-by their first, and in many cases their only impression of the building's purpose and character; and since it embodies the image that its occupiers project, it also provides an insight into the people who live and work there. This means that even those who merely cross the threshold are likely to assess the standing or success of a commercial organisation, or a private individual, on the basis of only a few glimpses.

But for the Chinese architect, the entrance has another vital function. In order that the building is filled with stimulating energies, the entrance, more than any other part of the building, must be constructed in accordance with the strictest principles of *Feng Shui*, since it can attract, or repel, the ever-vital *ch'i*. Indeed, when travellers to the Far East make their first encounter with *Feng Shui*, it is often because a remarkable feature in the design of the entrance to a building has caused comment.

The approach

The first principle is to avoid 'secret arrows' being directed at the entrance. For this reason, any path or driveway leading up to the entrance to a building should preferably follow a gentle curve, rather than making the direct straight approach which is often found both in grand and humbler buildings of European design. While there are many outstanding examples of Chinese architecture which have a formal avenue leading to the entrance, these invariably end in tiers of steps so that the 'secret arrows' are not directed at the entrance itself.

Entrances which lead directly on to a street without any approach path are generally considered to be unfavourable, too: and in such cases, if the entrance is placed in the centre of the front wall, the remedy is to set

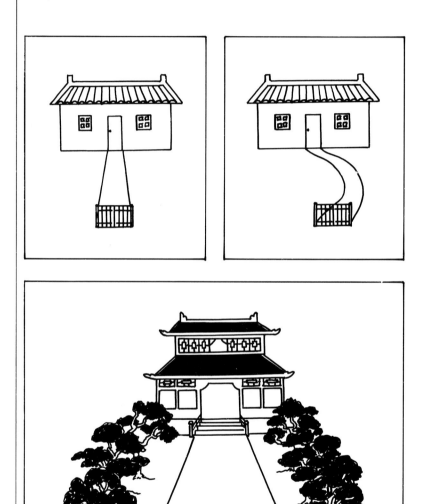

The Chinese favour a curved path to an entrance, thereby avoiding 'secret arrows'. More formal buildings may be approached by a straight avenue, but steps should be introduced to prevent the direct impact of unfavourable sha.

the entrance doors at an angle. (This ploy is so favoured by finance houses in South-East Asia that it is virtually a standard feature of bank architecture to find that the doors are either set at an angle, or positioned at the corner of the building.)

The way in

Throughout the world, house doors almost invariably open inwards. This is a reminder of times when a house was not just a shelter against wind and weather, but also had to be a sound defence against hostile attack. Doors which open inwards can be barricaded against unwelcome intruders.

According to *Feng Shui* theory, entrance doors are also required to open inwards because the door acts as a valve to beneficial *ch'i*, allowing these currents to pass into the house, but not out of it. (If the doors opened outwards, such good influences would escape without bringing benefit to the residents.)

In places where the climate is extreme, entrances are often provided with two sets of doors, so that there is a vestibule for conservation of either the central heating, or the air-conditioning: and whether the building is a

grand commercial concern with two sets of double doors, or a modest house with a glazed front porch, the same principles apply. Firstly, inner and outer doors should open in the same direction: and if a porch is to be built on to an existing house entrance, it should be ample enough to allow the outer door to open inwards into it – presuming, of course, that the house door also opens inwards, as it should. Secondly, both doors should open at the same side. If the porch door hangs on the left, and the house door on the right, this presents the visitor with a confusing impression at the threshold, perhaps subconsciously creating a negative or hostile reception, instead of a welcome.

Inner and outer doors should also line up exactly, or they should be distinctly separate. If the outer door cannot be fitted so that it exactly matches the position of the inner door, then it should be placed in such a way that it is obviously not meant to be in alignment. Pairs of doors which are slightly awry create a feeling of unease and disharmony.

If the occupier is a tenant, and unable to make any structural change to the fabric of the building by altering the positions of the doors, a simple solution is to fix a tall mirror, or a column of mirror tiles, alongside the inner door, on the side which faces the outer door overlap.

Study these various entrances, and determine which are favourable, according to Feng Shui theory. Doors should open inwards, remember, to allow beneficial ch'i to enter: and where there are two sets of doors, ideally they should line up, and open at the same side. If this cannot be, a mirror may provide a remedy. A direct path through the house is regarded as unfavourable, but drapes or a bead curtain will hide the rear exit. Stairs should not face the front door, but a mirror on the landing or, alternatively, curved lower steps will bring about more favourable Feng Shui by deflecting the route of the ch'i.

The Eight Trigrams

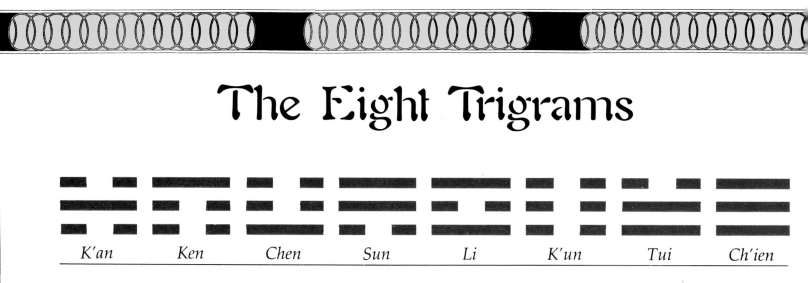

| K'an | Ken | Chen | Sun | Li | K'un | Tui | Ch'ien |

Once a building is completed, and the position of its entrance established, the location of the rooms has to be carefully considered. *Feng Shui* declares that the direction each room takes affects suitability for different purposes. For example, a West-facing room with tranquil qualities would be ideal for a lounge, but might prove too restful for a study or workshop; while a room highly receptive to stimulating and energizing currents could prove to be inappropriate for a bedroom.

A fascinating system, with origins cloaked by antiquity, is used to determine the innate *Feng Shui* qualities of each part of the house.

The system of the Eight Trigrams is taken from one of the oldest books in the Chinese or indeed any other language – a unique text known as the *I Ching*, or *Book of Changes*, regarded as a sacred, almost magical document. Each of the Eight Trigrams, which form the core of this remarkable work, consists of a combination of three solid or broken horizontal lines, representing *Yang*, the active force in nature, and *Yin*, the recessive force, respectively.

The ancient Chinese philosophers taught that these eight figures symbolize the creation of the whole of the natural and supernatural universe. Since together they represent the complete cosmos, they are considered to be a sure protection against evil forces. Accordingly, in Chinese houses, they can often be seen carved on the lintels, or hung up conspicuously in a hall or stairway.

The qualities of the trigram associated with each room will help to determine its most suitable purpose. The methods used to correlate the trigrams with the rooms of a house may involve three stages of complexity. At the most basic level, a trigram is allocated to a room which is most appropriate to its quality. Thus, for a bedroom in a single occupancy apartment, a *Tui* location would be a good choice, since *Tui* has the quality of serenity. Similarly, a kitchen might be placed in the *Li* (Fire and Heat) direction; and the dining-room in the *K'un* (Nourishment) position.

Then there is a second level which takes into account the trigram for each member of the family, as seen in the chart reproduced here. *Ch'ien*, for example, represents the father, kingship, and strength; and *Sun*, the eldest daughter, trade, and growth. Thus, each trigram is appropriate to a

Trigram Name		Emblem	Relationship	Quality	Direction
K'an	☵	Lakes	Middle son	Wheels, Danger	North
Ken	☶	Mountain	Youngest son	Obstacles	North-East
Chen	☳	Thunder	Eldest son	Speed, Roads	East
Sun	☴	Wind	Eldest daughter	Trade, Growth	South-East
Li	☲	Heat	Middle daughter	Fire, Heat	South
K'un	☷	Earth	Mother	Nourishment	South-West
Tui	☱	Sea	Youngest daughter	Joy, Serenity	West
Ch'ien	☰	Heaven	Father	Kingship	North-West

particular sphere of activity. In a family home, the master bedroom should be situated in the room ascribed to the *Ch'ien* trigram, while the eldest daughter's bedroom would be located at the *Sun* position. At a more detailed level, the professional geomancer would establish the positions of the Eight Trigrams from the owner's horoscope, using the method for matching the house to the horoscope described on pages 92-97.

Although they are directly associated with the Eight Directions – that is, the four cardinal points plus, as the Chinese call them, the four 'corners' (North-East, North-West, South-West, and South-East) - their association with specific directions varies. Of the thousands of ways in which the Eight Trigrams might be arranged, only two are commonly seen. The most usual arrangement found on talismanic mirrors, and at the centre of most types of *Lo P'an*, is called the 'Former Heaven' sequence, and has the *Ch'ien* trigram

(three unbroken lines) to represent South, depicted at the top. In the second arrangement – the 'Later Heaven' sequence used for mariners' compasses and certain types of *Lo P'an* – South, again traditionally at the top, is shown by the symbol *Li* (two full lines enclosing a broken one.) It is this arrangement by which the points of the compass are generally known: and though it is not as logical as the Former Heaven sequence, it is the one used in *Feng Shui* calculations. This Later Heaven sequence is the arrangement shown in the Direction column of the above chart.

But whatever direction the trigram represents, its meaning and name remain unchanged. So the three unbroken lines, *Ch'ien*, always represent the father, whether they appear at South or elsewhere.

It is difficult to translate the Chinese names owing to their antiquity, but they are always associated with certain emblems, as shown in the chart here.

Other entrances

If there are other entrances to the building, they should not be in line with the front door. Direct paths right through the house are thought to be highly unfavourable, since they conduct *ch'i* out of the house before the favourable currents have had time to circulate and distribute beneficial influences through the rooms of the building.

More obviously, a visitor's first impression of a house should be one of welcome, which is difficult to convey if the back door is immediately visible. On a more practical level, a passage running through the house tends to become a short cut from the front garden to the back, so imposing undue wear on the heart of the house. But perhaps more importantly, a central corridor should be avoided as it splits the house into two and is thought to have a potentially deleterious effect on the household. Intentionally or not, members of the family may resolve into two factions, subconsciously using the central passage as a demarcation line.

It follows that, where there is a central passageway through a house, every effort should be made to find the most practical means to block the back door, and if necessary, to have an alternative exit constructed, perhaps in the form of french windows leading from the living-room into the garden, or a door from the kitchen. The new exit should be made in a wall which is at right-angles to the front entrance. Of course, if these already exist, it would only be necessary to block the back door. The former passageway can then be transformed into an attractive and welcoming hallway.

There will be numerous occasions when it is not practical to carry out such reconstruction work. In such cases, every attempt should be made to destroy the impression of a central corridor. An interior door which divides the corridor would fulfil this purpose effectively. Alternatively, drapes or a bead curtain can be hung at a reasonable distance from the front door to obscure the view of the rear exit. It will then be possible to decorate and furnish the front part of the former corridor in such a way that the effect of an attractive and welcoming entrance hall is readily created.

Positioning the stairs

In houses of Western design, the entrance often leads into a hallway which has a staircase facing the door. *Feng Shui* theory declares that a staircase in this position destroys the network of *ch'i* in the building, and so such a lay-out would not be entertained in a traditional Chinese building under any circumstances. The favoured positioning is to have the staircase at right-angles to the entrance, or placed along another wall, out-of-sight of the entrance door. Of lesser importance is the rule that staircases should not be fitted in the middle of a building, which some authorities declare to be inauspicious.

Of course, it is no simple business to move a staircase; but it is sometimes possible to have the lowest treads turned, so that the bottom of the stairs is at an angle to the front door. If this is impossible, a drape, screen or bead curtain should be positioned between the staircase and the entrance to deflect the route of the *ch'i*. If space is very limited and there is no room for such a curtain, the traditional alternative is to fix a mirror to the wall at the top of the stairs; or, if there is a half-landing, to place there a protective guardian in the form of an ornamental dog, dragon, lion, or a figurine of one of the Chinese guardians.

The Living-room

Socially, the living-room is the focal point of the house. This is where the household gathers together, and where the family's personal treasures, reflecting their tastes, achievements, aspirations, and even social standing are displayed to all who are invited into the home. Family harmony may depend on this room's ability to evoke a happy domestic atmosphere, while *Feng Shui* traditions declare that, if beneficial *ch'i* are lacking from the heart of the house, the family will soon drift apart. In fact, those who find the surroundings uncomfortable may be led, even if subconsciously, to other places to relax – to other rooms in the house perhaps, or to a sympathetic ambience outside the home altogether: and after a while, the household, for no discernible reason, may find itself disintegrating.

In most households, there will be times when the living-room is called to serve a more formal function, playing the role of a reception room, since it is here that relatives will be received on important family occasions, and where neighbours, friends and perhaps business acquaintances are sometimes entertained. The family will want to make a favourable impression on older relatives; and those hoping to improve their career prospects may wish to impress their superiors, or clients. Thus it is essential for this room to be warm, welcoming, and filled with vitality. In a nutshell, for the household to prosper, the *Feng Shui* of the living room should be the most favourable possible.

Location and shape

If a new house is being built, several factors need to be taken into account when planning the location of the living-room: the direction it faces, and the positioning of doors, windows and fireplaces. When moving into an empty house, too, it is worth looking at these features in the light of the quality of their *Feng Shui*.

If the family follows Chinese tradition, and is fundamentally patriarchal, with the head of the household being both breadwinner and sole authority in the home, then the *Feng Shui* for the whole household will be planned according to the horoscope of this central figure. The geomancer, basing his calculations on the date of birth for the head of the household, will use the *Lo P'an* to determine what the functions of each room should be. (Detailed information on use of the *Lo P'an* can be found on pages 82-101 .) But when the family shares its responsibilities and decisions, it is important that a wider view should be taken.

Strictly speaking, considering how important the living-room is, it ought to face South; but any direction from West, through South, to East will be suitable, if not so favourable. Thought must also be given to the time of day when the room is most likely to be used. If it is to be

the morning, an Easterly view would be fine; and in the evening, a Westerly one, so that the shadow of the house will not be cast over the view.

According to *Feng Shui* principles, the best shape for any room is rectangular; but if the proposed living-room is L-shaped or irregular, the largest rectangular area available can be created by dividing the space with a partition of some kind, or by placing a screen in position to form the fourth side of a rectangle.

Walls and doors

Ideally, there will be one plain, unbroken wall – that is, without doors or windows – but it may be that any screen or partition will have to function as the unbroken wall. If there is a fireplace, this should be positioned in the unbroken wall. Alternatively, in order to enable favourable *ch'i* to flow round the room, one of the best situations for the fireplace is the same wall that has the main door into the room.

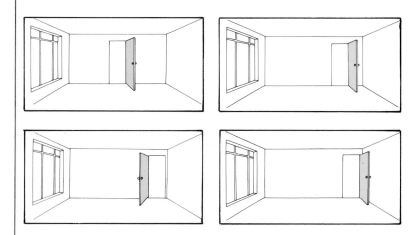

Which is the most favoured position for the door in a living-room, and how should it open? Feng Shui principles state that it should either be placed centrally along one wall, and with its hinge away from a window; or at a point one-seventh the length of that wall from one end, with its hinge next to the wall. Keep the space behind the door to a minimum, too, lest ch'i be allowed to get stale. The wall opposite the door should be unbroken, providing an ideal opportunity to display some item of interest which will attract attention on entering.

The door which leads into the room should open inwards to the most spacious area, indicating a welcome, and should either be placed centrally, or – in a very large room – at a point one-seventh the length of the wall from one end. If the door is at the end of the wall, it should open with the hinge next to the adjoining wall. A central door, however, should open with the hinge on the side away from a window. Whether or not the door's position is ideal, consideration should also be given to the area immediately in front of the door, which should be as clear as possible. Care should be taken, too, that space behind the opened door is kept to a minimum so that the *ch'i* are not allowed to stagnate. This principle may have arisen from a fear that intruders may lurk there.

Ideally the wall opposite the door will be the unbroken one, as this provides an opportunity to place something of interest in such a position that it catches the eye immediately the door is opened. But aggressive items – swords, guns, and hunting trophies, for example – are best positioned on the entrance door wall. The aim is to excite the visitor's curiosity, not apprehension.

Doors which lead from the room into other parts of the house, or french windows leading into a garden, should open away from the room. French windows, or any other exterior doors, should be considered as 'exit' doors, lockable from the inside only, and admitting entry only when they are left open for the convenience of the company then present.

The Chinese geomancer would further advise his client that windows and doors should not face each other; and in particular, that windows should not be in opposite walls. The 'see-through' living-room does not find favour in the Chinese scheme of things. Such rooms have no stable focal point: and there is neither a sense of movement round the room, nor a point of repose. Two opposing vistas create an uncomfortable feeling: and, watching the view from one window, the observer may be conscious of and concerned about something happening behind. If doors and windows do face each other, however, some intervening feature ought to break up the direct line. Plants, room-dividers, or drapes will serve this purpose effectively.

Doors and windows may admit *ch'i* into the room,

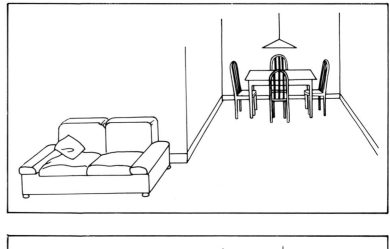

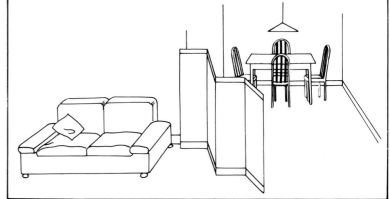

The L-shaped living-room is not highly favoured; and, according to Feng Shui tenets, should be divided into two distinct areas, by a screen, perhaps.

but the fireplace conducts it away. In guiding the *ch'i* round the room, mirrors deflect beneficial currents, and also help to bring light to difficult corners. (It is an interesting thought that some underlying *Feng Shui* instinct may have led to the common Western practice of placing large mirrors above fire-places. However, a fire-place may also have the positive effect of absorbing unfavourable *sha*, if they strike the wall at that point, in which case a mirror would be counter-productive.)

In warmer climates, consideration can also be given to the positioning of electric fans, as those will move the air, guiding the *ch'i* around the room.

The Symbolism of Colour

For more than two thousand years, the Chinese have always paid great regard to the symbolism of colour. Indeed, the Five Elements – Wood, Fire, Earth, Metal, and Water – are associated with their own five special colours: blue-green, red, yellow, white, and black. The first colour, *Ch'ing* (associated with the Wood Element), is used to refer either to the blue of the sky, or the green of plants, as it seems the ancient Chinese made no distinction between these shades. However, for red, associated with Fire, and life, there are several different words in Chinese, all interchangeable. Red is also regarded as the 'lucky' colour by the Chinese, which is why messages of congratulations, New Year and birthday cards, wedding invitations and the like are always printed on red paper.

Yellow – associated with the Element Earth – is the ochre colour of the silt which gives the Yellow River its name.

Interestingly, the Chinese word for yellow, *Huang*, has the same sound as the word for 'royal', and was used as the Imperial colour by the Manchus; while in the elaborate ornamentation of temples and palaces, the colour yellow is often represented by gold decoration.

The Metal Element is symbolized by white, recalling the glint of iron or silver. The elemental colour is therefore not so much a pure white as a silvery grey. (In China, white – the symbol of purity – is a funereal colour, and so usually avoided in ornamentation.)

Black, the colour of the Water Element, is actually considered to be a lucky colour by many Chinese, who associate it with money. However, modern Chinese, influenced by Western custom, may hold it in the same regard as Westerners, and associate it with the macabre.

According to *Feng Shui* principles, when it is impractical to make any structural changes to a room or building, a judicious use of the five colours can balance a preponderance or deficiency of a particular Element.

In general, the colour scheme for a room should be chosen according to the direction it faces. For example, a geomancer, having examined a house with a North-facing entrance, would probably advise the occupants to re-paint a red front gate black. The reasoning would be that, as red represents Fire, and North corresponds to the Element Water, the Water and Fire would cause conflict.

The colours of the first three Elements (blue-green, red, and yellow) in their primary state are too garish and theatrical to be used as interior decoration in a family home, but they can easily be toned down to suit even the most conservative of tastes. Green, blue and turquoise tones, suggesting growth and harmony, are appropriate for East-facing rooms; red tints and pinks to rooms which face the South; and autumnal yellows and ochres to rooms facing West. For North-facing rooms which need as much light as possible, pale colours are advisable, with the odd, bold contrast of black.

In the other rooms, when a contrasting colour is required as part of the decoration, it should be one which precedes or follows the dominant colour, in the *productive* order of the Five Elements, as given on page 89.

To remedy adverse *Feng Shui* situations, it is often the practice of professional geomancers to take into account the Element of the direction, and to recommend use of a colour associated with the Element preceding it in the *productive* order.

If the ideal *Feng Shui* combination of colours conflicts with taste, it is usually sufficient to have token use of the appropriate colour in an ornament or item of furniture.

Arrangement of furniture

Whether the *Feng Shui* of the living-room is ideal, or whether it is unimpressive or frankly undesirable, there will always be certain areas and locations which will be more favourable than others: and in positioning the furniture, every opportunity can be taken to correct whatever defects may exist, and to enhance whatever positive qualities there are.

In general, Chinese taste favours a very formal arrangement of furnishings for a reception room. For example, in a rectangular room, the neatest form of

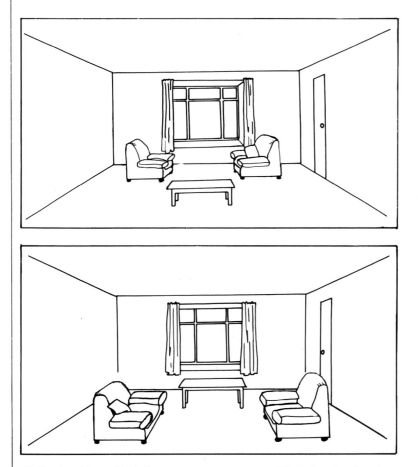

Following Feng Shui theory, a geomancer would advise that furniture in the living-room should be arranged to follow the lines of the four walls, and so that no chairs directly face nor have the back to a window or a door.

presentation is to place chairs and small tables squarely so that they follow the lines of the four walls, forming an internal rectangle.

Good *Feng Shui* demands that furniture be set out so that no chairs are either directly facing, nor with their backs to the doors or windows. People naturally feel more secure with solid walls behind them, and those who are in the room will want to see who is coming to the door.

The *Feng Shui* geomancer will advise placing your furniture so that beneficial currents are able to flow through the room without stagnating. A good rule-of-thumb is to imagine a path meandering through the room without leaving any vacant plots, entering and leaving at the most favourable points. If there is a second door leading from the room to another part of the house, the *ch'i* should be guided to it; otherwise, conduct the *ch'i* to leave by the window.

Tradition also holds that seating should not be placed under overhead features, particularly beams, such as those found in older, country properties, as well as hi-tech buildings. Apart from the obvious danger to tall people when rising, Chinese observers maintain that there is a psychological factor, and that overhead beams tend to cause headaches in those sitting below them.

Honoured guests should be seated in the master's position, normally facing South.

Windows and views

Where there is a window, there is also a view, and it should be a pleasant one. It may be that a natural landscape provides the attractive aspect; or alternatively that the window looks out to a finely designed garden. In either case, it is ideal for water, a lake, a mountain stream, fountain or humble pond to be visible.

But if the view is unattractive, and nothing can be done to improve it, every attempt should be made to draw attention away from the window by using some interior feature of the room as a major focal point of interest, while the windows themselves can be veiled by blinds or screening curtains. These become of even greater importance if there are 'secret arrows' outside, pointing at the window. They should be countered by establishing a neutralising Element in the room. This can be done in one of two ways. To counterbalance life-draining *sha*, the Chinese often employ fish tanks, especially tanks containing red goldfish. Several reasons have been given to account for the universal fondness for these particular fish bowls. Apart from its aesthetic value, it is said that the bowl of water acts as the *Ming T'ang* or reservoir which is able to absorb the hurt from the 'secret arrow'. Furthermore, as the red colour of the fish represents the Element Fire, the surrounding water suggests that the premises are protected against fire. Many Chinese also believe that the fish, being live, are able to stimulate beneficial *ch'i* through their movement and vitality. What is indisputable is that a well-kept tank of fish is a restful and soothing focal point.

The alternative method used for counterbalancing any inauspicious features involves the use of the *Lo P'an*, and is described in detail in Example 2 on page 92. This method is frequently used by geomancers of the Compass school.

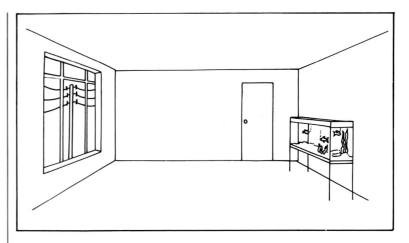

A simple fish tank is one traditional way of neutralising the effect of threatening sha – from an inauspicious telegraph pole, for instance.

The Dining-room

Chinese cuisine is not designed for the lone eater. In the Far East, the notable feature of Chinese restaurants (those, that is, that cater for Chinese communities) and one that makes them so markedly different from restaurants in the Western world, is their sheer size. Vast, brilliantly decorated halls accommodate rank after rank of huge tables, round which family parties of a dozen or more will feast together – a far cry from the intimate atmosphere of a dimly-lit French or Italian restaurant. Nor do the Chinese delicately keep to their own plates. Etiquette demands that a meal be shared, and that each person at the table should sample all the various dishes that are set down.

Travelling in China, when I have entered a restaurant alone, I have frequently been pressed to join a party of people who until then would have been complete strangers, to share their company and their meal. Thus,

eating at the table not only nourishes the body, it also symbolizes friendship, and harmony.

Within the home, however, the placing of the dining-room is not as crucial as the location of other rooms. But it is ideal for the dining-room to be East of the kitchen, failing which, it might be placed to the South of it.

Favourable *ch'i* are encouraged if the dining-room window faces a different direction from the section of the house where the room is situated, provided that this is not its opposite. That is to say, if the dining-room is located in the Southern part of the house, it is favourable for the window to face Eastwards; or if in the Eastern part, Southwards. If the dining-room is in the North, the windows should look East or West; and if in the West, North or South.

Ch'i should not rest and stagnate in the dining-room, or the atmosphere will become stale and unpleasant. Consequently, it is preferable that there should be at least two entrances to the dining-room, one from the hallway or living-room, and another from the direction of the kitchen. For the same reason, it is also best if there are at least two windows. The two doors should also be in the same wall, or in adjacent walls, as should the windows. Doors opposite each other are not favoured, as this creates the impression of a corridor, rather than a room.

Furnishing the dining-room

The essential furnishings of any dining-room are its table and chairs. A round table symbolizes Heaven, harmony, and friendship, while a square table, representing the Earth, suggests a more formal, hierarchical approach. Octagonal tables are often found in China, since each side faces one of the Eight Directions.

Despite the apparent informality of the round table, any honoured guest, or the eldest member of the family, should be placed at the North side of the table, so as to face the South. At an eight-sided table, the family should be disposed according to the Eight Trigrams, as indicated by the chart on page 41.

Apart from the sideboard, the remaining furnishings should be minimal. Unless the dining-room serves a double purpose as the living-room or a second reception room, there is little need for other furniture, which would only intrude on the principal focus: the table.

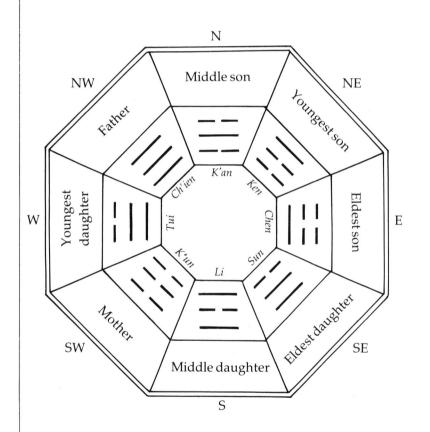

At an octagonal table, highly favoured in China, the family should be seated according to the Eight Trigrams, with the father at the North-West position and mother at the South-West. The eldest son will be seated at the East, the middle son at the North, and the youngest son at the North-East. The eldest daughter takes her place at the South-East, the middle daughter at the South, and the youngest daughter at the West.

The Kitchen

The very nature of the kitchen sets it apart from all the other rooms in the household. Here, the Elements Fire and Water are combined; and though heating may be supplied throughout the house, and water in the bathroom and lavatory, the two Elements do not come into collision as they do in the kitchen. Another Element is evident, too – Metal: and in the role of the utensils, it has the function of separating Fire from Water. Traditional kitchens – particularly in country houses – use wood-burning stoves; but since most fuels are ultimately derived from vegetation, either recent or fossil, the fuel consumed by the stove is considered to be represented by the Element Wood. Thus, the kitchen is a microcosm of the four directional Elements: Wood for the East, Fire for the South, Metal for the West, and Water for the North. Only the Element Earth, which represents the centre, is missing.

In primitive houses of the past, especially those in cold Northern climates, the stove and central chimney usually stood at the centre of the house, for this was the most economic way to conserve fuel and to heat the house. From the point of view of *Feng Shui*, the centre of the house was also the ideal situation for the kitchen, since the centre represented the absent Earth Element. In modern times, however, most houses adopt the practice suited to more temperate climates, where a central stove would make the house unbearably hot in summer, by siting the stove and chimney, if indeed there is a chimney, on the outside walls.

If the kitchen is not centrally situated, *Feng Shui* practitioners generally agree that it should be sited away from the entrance. Having the kitchen next to the entrance may well give the visitor the impression that the family's prime consideration is food, which hints at greed. Furthermore, the entrance, if ideally situated, will be on the South-facing side of the house, which is associated with Fire. Since the kitchen generates fire, this direction ought to be avoided, otherwise there could be a superabundance of this Element, creating danger within the house itself. Putting the kitchen in the North would emphasize the Element Water. But Water destroys Fire, also creating an unfavourable situation. The presence of Metal, however, acts as a controlling Element. It is neither produced, like Fire, nor consumed, like Water, but remains unchanged. Metal is associated with the West, so that a Western location for the kitchen is the very best *Feng Shui* solution.

If the kitchen is located in the North part of the house, however, a West-facing window or outside door will improve the flow of *ch'i*, which can then leave through the most appropriate direction.

A West-facing kitchen has the best Feng Shui, but the correct placing of items within the kitchen is also important. There should, for instance, be an intervening Element between the stove and the water supply. Which arrangement is therefore most preferable?

Fitting the kitchen

Within the kitchen, various features should be placed in their most appropriate relative positions. The stove, for example, should be placed on the South side, according to its ruling Element, Fire. There must also be an intervening Element between the stove and the water supply. So on the left of the stove should be something pertaining to the Elements Wood or Metal. For example, if the stove burns solid fuel, the intervening space would be the proper location for the wood-basket or coal-scuttle; if the stove burns gas or electricity, use the space for storing metal utensils. The fourth wall will then be used for storage space, and the refrigerator/freezer.

Adjoining rooms

An old rule of *Feng Shui*, which is echoed by many Western planning authorities, is that the kitchen should not be situated next to the bathroom or lavatory. But such a regulation is often impracticable, since the position of these rooms will be determined by the access to a mains water supply and drainage. If the kitchen and the bathroom/lavatory are likely to be close to each other, there should either be a passage between the two rooms;

or failing that, a store-room or cupboard. If it is absolutely impossible to avoid the two rooms being adjacent, then the kitchen wall which backs on to the bathroom must *not* be the one which houses the stove, and preferably should be opposite it. Putting the bathroom above the kitchen (a common Western practice) is considered extremely bad *Feng Shui* because waste will flow past a vital area.

In some houses, the kitchen also doubles as a family dining-room. In these cases, the two functions should be clearly separated; one area for the cooking and preparation, and another for eating. It is not favourable for the dining-table to be placed at the centre of the kitchen,

The Kitchen Guardian

In Chinese houses, the kitchen is dignified by its own guardian spirit, *Tsao Wang*. He is the 'King of the Stove' and watches over the family throughout the year, to protect them in times of danger, also taking note of their wrong-doings, and reporting these to the judges of the other world at the end of the year. A week before the New Year, his paper image is taken down and ceremoniously burnt, usually with a little straw for his horse, and sweets or a little honey for himself, to persuade him to forget some of the family's ill-deeds. If the family feel particularly guilty for any reason, they might go so far as to dip the effigy in brandy before burning it, so that by the time *Tsao Wang* reaches the celestial judgement hall, he will be too drunk to remember his mission! A week later, on New Year's Day, a fresh picture is pasted up so that the King of the Stove can resume his duties.

surrounded by activities and implements. Nor, according to *Feng Shui* principles, should those eating a meal sit at side tables, facing the walls or windows, with their backs to the centre, as this totally destroys the harmony of the household. Instead, the dining-area should be to the East or South of the cooking and preparation area, since the East represents the Element Wood, symbol of growth and nourishment; and the South, good fortune and harmony.

The Study

Any room which is reserved for study should be both quiet and peaceful, yet mentally stimulating. An area which is too restful may lead to the studies being abandoned through drowsiness, while an atmosphere which is too saturated in stimulating *ch'i* may cause the reader to become agitated, so that there is a temptation to quit the tranquillity of the study for a more vigorous pastime of some kind.

Ch'i should therefore flow gently through the room. In practice, any room used for a study will be filled with cupboards, bookcases, antiquities, and other revered objects. These not only help to slow down the passage of the *ch'i*, they also act as a secondary barrier to the world outside, blocking off all the distractions of everyday life, and helping to deaden extraneous sounds.

The actual centre of study, however, should be as spacious as possible, like a deep pool in a river where the water flows imperceptibly, and where the *ch'i* can accumulate before flowing away. Here, at the heart of the room, there should be ample unoccupied space for the eye, and consequently the mind, to rest upon. There is no harm in having a protective wall of useful reference files and working material, but within its confines there must be horizontal surfaces which are always kept clear of clutter. If a table is by a window, the person seated should be placed sideways to the window. The only exception to this is if the window faces North, when it is possible to sit facing the window.

The study should be gently, not harshly lit, and for that reason may face North, particularly because this is also the direction associated with Water, the Element of communication and study. Colours in this room may be generally dark-toned, as it is likely that only one spot, the desk, will need to be well lit. A desk by a North-facing window is ideally situated, since the light is diffused, and will not cause glare.

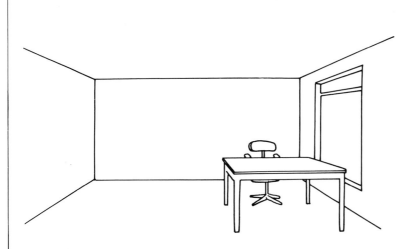

In the study, a desk should be placed sideways to a window, and the very centre of the room ought to be as spacious and clear as possible.

Borrowed natural light – that is, light which does not enter the room directly – is also acceptable, provided that it is adequate: that is, there should be enough to judge the time of day during daylight hours. For reading and close work, of course, it will probably still be necessary to have supplementary lighting by the desk.

Chinese scholars customarily have a carved pen stand, ink slab, or seal in the shape of a mountain on their desks. Although the carving is considered to be a focal point for their contemplation, the practice of having a model mountain on the desk actually follows the teachings of the Form school of *Feng Shui*, which advocates the proximity of a Dragon in the landscape.

Other *Feng Shui* objects, such as mirrors, fish, and plants, are not entirely appropriate to the study, however.

Mirrors reflect energizing *ch'i*, which are more suited to stimulating physical activity; and fish and plants, being live and therefore needing attention, may ultimately prove to be a hindrance rather than a help.

The Bedroom

After the entrance, *Feng Shui* regards the master bedroom as the most important room in the house. After all, this is where the householders will spend more than a third of their lives, at a time when they are at their most vulnerable, and in greatest need of protection from natural and supernatural agencies. As a consequence, there are more popular adages concerning the *Feng Shui* of the bedroom than for any other part of the house.

If building has not yet progressed beyond the planning stage, then it will be possible for the orientation of the master bedroom to be related directly to the house-owner's personal horoscope. Since the bedroom is the most personal room in the house, it is the one room which, more than any other, should be compatible with the features of the horoscope chart. How the *Feng Shui* masters do this is explained in detail on page 93.

Thus, a *Feng Shui* consultant will, at the earliest planning stages, advise the architect on the location of the master bedroom. His suggestions will take into account the orientation which is most favourable to the client, while incorporating other considerations, such as tranquillity and view. If, for example, the client was born in the year of the Rat, associated with the North direction, but the North aspect overlooks a main and noisy road, it would be possible to plan the bedroom so that its location is Northerly, with its windows giving a view to the East or West, and with the bed against the Northerly wall.

A bedroom with an East-facing window will be greeted by the morning sun filling the room with vitality, at a time when it is most needed. The bed itself, however, should not be placed in the path of the sun's beams, for it

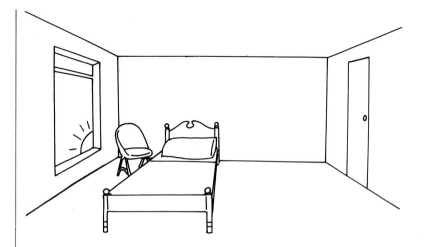

Ideally, the bed should not be by a window: but if this is unavoidable, space should be left for a chair or table.

is said to be better for the first sight of morning to be viewed aslant. If the room has a West-facing window, the sun will not reach the room until late evening. This may prove relaxing and conducive to a good night's rest, but it will not provide a particularly invigorating start to the day. Such a situation might be suitable, however, for the elderly or retired, or those needing to convalesce. There is no advantage in the bedroom having a South-facing window, since the sun will fill the room when it is vacant. A North-facing room, which does not face the sun, might provide splendid views of the winter sky, but the subdued morning light could perhaps prove a rather depressing start to the day.

But these are not the only considerations which either affect, or are determined by, the bedroom's position. It is also important that the bedroom is not located over an empty but enclosed space, such as a storeroom. The *Feng Shui* explanation is that such dark and unventilated places do not permit the *ch'i* to circulate freely. Thus, a stagnant area of dead *ch'i* may be created beneath the sleeper, leading to psychological discomfiture which may ultimately develop into some form of physical illness.

In effect, this also means that bedrooms should not be built over garages. Despite the sensibility of this basic *Feng Shui* principle, many modern houses in the Western hemisphere are in notorious breach of it. Yet the inherent dangers ought to be self-evident: inflammable materials, by necessity kept in garages, pose a threat of fire, while there is a real possibility that chronic poisoning may result from the continual breathing (about three thousand hours every year) of toxic vapours seeping into the bedroom.

Often, in order to take advantage of a spectacular view, hotels or houses on hillsides will have rooms built on terraces or projecting jetties. Despite scenic views, these rooms should not be designated as master bedrooms. Here, where there is a superabundance of energizing *ch'i*, the sleeper, feeling perched on a precipice, may be subconsciously aware of potential danger; and, on waking, may not feel wholly rested. Short-stay visitors and the young might take advantage of the energising *ch'i* for a few days; but exposure to such vital influences for longer periods could prove exhausting.

It is best for the bedroom to have one entrance, and to be approached from a corridor, rather than for it to adjoin another room. If it must do so, it is better for the adjoining room to be one with slow-moving *ch'i*. In other words, the adjoining room should be another bedroom, a dressing-room, the living-room, or study, and not the kitchen or a games room. Despite the convenience of an en suite bathroom, this is not favourable according to the principles of *Feng Shui*. The objection is to the presence of water in close proximity to the sleeper. Whatever may have been the reasoning of the ancient scholars, it is true that adjacent bathrooms, with their attendant gurglings and rumblings, are a frequent source of irritation. Therefore, it is advisable to separate the bathroom from the bedroom either with an intervening corridor, a built-in wardrobe, or adequate insulation. In essence, the bedroom should be the last call of the *ch'i* through the house. *Ch'i* should enter softly, and leave just as quietly.

Location of the bed

In positioning the bed in the room, the main stipulation is that it should not face the door. Indeed, the Chinese feel decidedly uneasy if the door faces the foot of the bed,

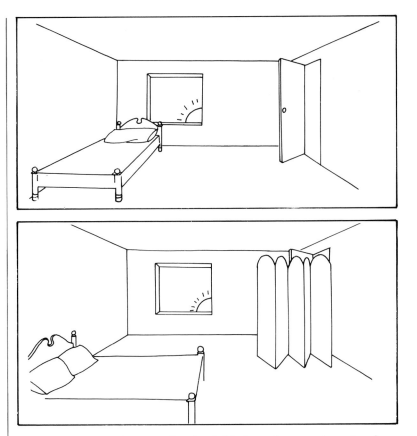

The bed should not be immediately visible from the open door. In a large room, a screen will not only preserve modesty and prevent draughts, but also channel the flow of ch'i to good effect.

since this is associated with the funeral custom of laying the deceased with feet to the door, so that the spirit may have easier access to Heaven; and more practically, to help the mourners carry the body through the door. In small rooms, the bed should be placed against a wall, not against a window; but if having the bed parallel with the window is unavoidable, there should be a gap, allowing room for a chair or a bedside table.

The door itself should also open in such a way that the bed is not immediately visible. This principle probably arose because there were occasions when servants, members of the family or visitors might enter the bedroom and surprise its occupants in a state of undress; while if a door acted as a screen, it would give a second or two for a warning to be signalled.

When the bedroom is large enough to warrant it, a screen can be placed in front of the door. This will guard modesty, keep away draughts, and furthermore serve the *Feng Shui* purpose of deflecting the flow of *ch'i* – not completely impeding this current but channeling it into a gentle rather than an energising one. In the ideal position, the door should be sideways to the bed.

Feng Shui geomancers also advise that the bed should never be situated under a sloping ceiling or a beam. If, as in a garret room, a sloping ceiling cannot be avoided, the bed should be positioned so that the plane of the slope follows the length of the bed, not its breadth. The same rule applies to beams. If these are a prominent feature of the room, do not let them traverse the bed, as it is believed they may cause illness in that part of the body which lies beneath the beam.

In some rooms, mirrors are an advantage, as they conduct *ch'i* round the room. In the bedroom, however, they are less useful. They are important for dressing, but they should be very carefully positioned so that they are not facing the bed. Indeed, the Chinese believe that the sleeper's spirit would take fright at seeing its own reflection. Furthermore, when positioning the mirror, while it might be a decided advantage to see who is about to enter, those at the door may also see the sleeper, a matter which intending burglars and sneak thieves may find extremely helpful. Completely mirrored walls and ceilings are not advantageous either: they may be considered by some to be chic, but by stimulating the flow of energising *ch'i*, they are neither soothing nor restful.

The Bathroom

As might be expected, both the bathroom and lavatory are associated with the Element Water, which belongs to the North direction. As a consequence, the Northern side of the house will be the most suitable location for them. The purpose of the bathroom and lavatory is to cleanse the body, externally and internally; and for this reason, the *ch'i* should be encouraged to flow through quickly and not allowed to settle or stagnate. According to Chinese tradition, elaborate bathrooms, which inhibit the flow of *ch'i*, should therefore be avoided.

No matter how small the bathroom, according to *Feng Shui* principles, there should be a window leading to the outside. This is not merely for ventilation. Despite the fact that modern extractor fans can cope adequately with the problems of keeping the air fresh – possibly even more efficiently than natural ventilation – if the bathroom or lavatory does not have one exterior wall, it follows that the room is situated in the core of the building, a feature which is highly undesirable. In traditional Chinese houses, the central area was an enclosed courtyard, which had an almost sacred function. Not even trees were allowed to occupy the centre, and it would certainly be considered extremely disagreeable to have the bathroom or lavatory there. If, however, the bathroom is centrally placed, it should be abundantly provided with mirrors, if possible on each wall.

As the bathroom, lavatory and kitchen need to be situated close to the water mains and drainage systems, it may be expedient to have the bathroom and kitchen close together, but they should not be adjacent. *Feng Shui* also declares that the bathroom/lavatory should never lead into or from the bedroom, as their *Feng Shui* qualities are not compatible.

Water should not be seen flowing away; thus waste pipes, overflows, and drains should be covered or concealed. Many Chinese bathrooms, instead of baths or showers, have floor-mounted sinks and scoops with which water is poured over the body. This method of bathing conserves water. Interestingly, although there is no shortage of

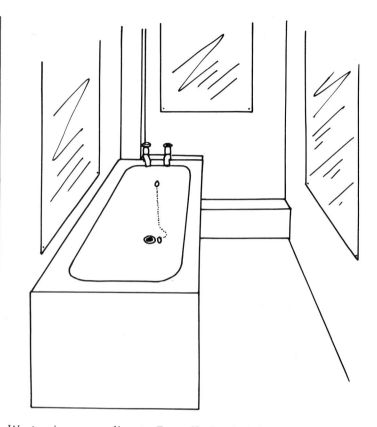

Waste pipes, according to Feng Shui principles, should be concealed wherever possible; while a centrally-sited bathroom, with no windows, should be liberally provided with mirrors to improve the Feng Shui.

water in South-East Asia, wasting water infers financial waste. (In Chinese, *Shui* – water – is a slang term for money.)

Unless the bathroom or lavatory has high walls, with a glass ceiling and several windows, any open space should not be obscured by potted plants. These may obstruct the flow of the *ch'i*, encourage staleness, and so create unhealthy stagnant areas.

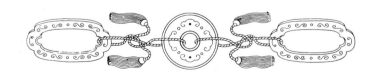

Magic Mirrors

Mirrors are among the most common remedies used to correct adverse *Feng Shui* situations.

They have a long and respected history in China, and are even known to have been worn, slung from the girdle cord, as early as the seventh century BC. But they were not mere accessories to personal grooming: rather, their mysterious power of reflection, revealing a parallel world beyond the surface, was regarded as magical. The mirrors themselves were considered to be models of the universe, and the backs were frequently decorated with astrological designs and inscriptions.

In *Feng Shui*, their use is largely intuitive: for while they may be disposed to encourage the flow of beneficial *ch'i* round a room, they may just as readily be employed to deflect harmful *sha* back to source.

Again, the power of mirrors to put the inhabitants of the invisible world to flight can act for good or evil. When positioning them to protect the house from the entry of threatening spirits, therefore, care has to be taken that they are not so placed that they are likely to alarm the soul of a sleeper when it rises for nocturnal wanderings.

Though mirrors might terrify the souls of the living, they were regarded as indispensible for the soul on its journey after life: and because of the ancient custom of burying mirrors with the dead, hundreds of handsome examples of bronze mirrors have survived the centuries.

Mirrors, too, are regarded as symbols of a long and happy marriage. At a wedding, for example, a mirror will sometimes be introduced so that rays of fortunate light are reflected upon the bride; and the death of a spouse is often compared with a broken mirror.

In business, a mirror placed behind a cash register is believed to have effect of increasing profits. At home, meanwhile, a small mirror by a bed is also thought to be effective in warding off evil spirits or intruders who, on entering, would see their reflections and be frightened away.

Certain *Feng Shui* practitioners also hold that mirrors should not be hung too high. Nor should they be placed so low that the tallest member of the family cannot see his whole face, or headaches may result.

But there are some mirrors with properties even more remarkable than any symbolic, or even supernatural power they were deemed to possess. These particular mirrors, of white bronze, had the astonishing ability to reflect the design embossed on the back, as if the solid bronze had become transparent in some unfathomable way – an effect which defies all rational scientific explanation. It is hardly surprising that these mirrors should be credited with supernatural powers. Indeed, what could be a surer talisman than something which was so obviously the threshold between the physical and immortal worlds?

PART FOUR
The Work-place

How the Perfect Direction
creates Prosperity

Madam Lang hurled the silk embroidery to the ground.

"That's the best place for floor cloths!" she snapped at the unfortunate girl, humiliating her before moving on to inspect the work of her companions. She was not in one of her better moods, having again arrived a couple of hours later than the team she was supposed to supervise, and making up for her shortcomings by bullying the girls.

"Is that all you've managed to do today?" she snorted. "As soon as I'm away on business, trying to find enough work to occupy you simpletons, you spend all your time in idle gossip". To emphasize her point, she took up another piece of embroidery, one that had taken the girl the whole of two days to complete, and ripped it in two.

The girl looked at the torn silk in disbelief. Ignoring her silent tears, Madam Lang edged towards Pei-Yu, one of the senior girls, whose work was always exquisite, and picked up a handsome dragon and phoenix wedding shawl, which Pei-Yu had only just completed.

"This is coming along quite well," Madam Lang volunteered. "But it still needs a little more work. Carry on with your present piece; I'll see to this one." And she hurried to her office with the shawl.

Madam Lang took a needle and began to unpick Pei-Yu's mark. She winced as, clumsy as always, she let the needle prick her finger. She hated embroidery as much as she detested her old fool of a brother-in-law. But she had taken this position at the factory for the same reason that she had married into the family: money, or at least, the promise of it.

She still had the needle and the shawl in her hands when Mr Eng burst in.

"Ah, dear sister-in-law, busy as ever, I see." He picked up the shawl admiringly. "Such beautiful craftsmanship." Madam Lang cast her eyes downwards in feigned modesty.

"What a delicate touch you have, my dear. No one else can match your skill. If only the girls could produce more work of this quality, then we could all be rich. Heaven bless you for your loyalty."

"That is my pleasure, dear brother-in-law. Indeed, if only there were enough hours in the day, I would gladly sit here, sewing for you. But you know, someone has to watch over these idle maids, see to the orders, and do the accounts for you. Or where would you be?"

"Considerably richer," thought the porter, Cheng, bitterly, as he overheard the conversation.

Cheng wasn't so concerned about his employer, Mr Eng, losing money, as the fact that Madam Lang was swindling him. Sometimes, too, the way she treated the girls made him tremble with rage. But though he loathed her, no less than the sewing-girls did, there was nothing he could do. Mr Eng was so besotted by his sister-in-law that he would refuse to believe that he was being mercilessly cheated.

Cheng knew several of Madam Lang's tricks, but suspected that it was only half of them. The pieces that Madam Lang didn't palm off on Mr Eng as her own work, she would sell to another merchant in the town. The accounts office, by the entrance, made it so very convenient to come and go, as the fancy took her, that it was very simple to take with her the odd 'unfinished' piece, the 'spoilt' cloths, and the 'inferior' work when she went on one of her jaunts to town. It would be a pleasure to see Mr Eng become a millionaire, if only to see Madam Lang get her just desserts.

It was a few days later, when Mr Eng had called Cheng into his own office for the usual weekly report, that an absent-minded remark was to change the course of all their fortunes.

As usual, Mr Eng was haranguing his porter about falling profits; but this time, he had half-heartedly asked the porter if he had any notions as to how the efficiency of the workshop might be improved.

Cheng suddenly had an idea. Without pausing to think, he replied: "Perhaps you should engage a *Feng Shui* professor." He stopped abruptly, shocked at his own impertinence. Mr Eng looked up sharply.

"I beg your pardon, Mr Eng," Cheng stammered. "It's not my place to advise you on such things. I'm sorry." Mr Eng angrily dismissed Cheng with a wave of his hand. Later, however, he called him back.

"You understand, Cheng, that I don't put great store by such matters. But do you happen to know of anyone who practises *Feng Shui* round here? Not too expensive, you realise. Someone who might advise for a modest fee. . . ."

Cheng did his best to conceal a smile. "As a matter of fact, Sir, I do."

Cheng's cousin, Kung, was regarded as the clever one in the family. But one thing he wasn't good at was making money: so whatever retainer he might get from Cheng's boss would be very welcome indeed. Mr Eng wasn't impressed by the geomancer's youth, even though he seemed to know many of the classics by heart. But as Cheng pointed out, being only an apprentice, he wouldn't cost so much. Perhaps, he suggested, the student might be happy with just a couple of silver taels. Mr Eng winced.

Somewhat nervously, Kung cleared his throat, and pointed at the entrance. "The entrance faces East. This belongs to the symbol *Chen*, and is concerned with all matters to do with movement and roads. That means it is indeed a good place to have the entrance."

Mr Eng stared at him blankly. "So?"

Cousin Kung was silent for a moment; then he stepped towards the workshop. "Your workshop faces the South-East. This belongs to the symbol *Sun*, and is concerned with work and trade. And also ladies. This is therefore a good place for the ladies to work."

"Indeed?" said Mr Eng, impassively.

They moved to Mr Eng's office. "Your office is placed in the direction North-West, which represents the symbol *Ch'ien*, concerned with the head of the concern, and management. This is an ideal place for your office."

Mr Eng threw a frosty glance at Cheng. "So there is nothing wrong with the *Feng Shui* of my establishment?"

"Ah." Cousin Kung took a deep breath, and then announced: "Unfortunately, Mr Eng, your accounts office is not favourably situated. I can see the practical reasons for having the office where it is, but it is at present in the direction North-East, associated with the symbol *Ken*. This concerns gate-keepers, and is a masculine symbol. It would be much better for this place to be occupied by a man, perhaps, er . . . a porter.

"At the same time, I notice that, close to your own office, there is a room in the West position, at the symbol *Tui*, at present occupied by your porter. But this signifies young ladies, serenity, and joy. Perhaps such a place would be better occupied by the revered lady who is your present book-keeper."

It did not take long for Mr Eng to realise the full implications of such an exchange.

"But would such a position, so close to my own office, be seemly?" he asked. "Indeed," replied the student, calmly. "It would be most proper."

Despite his sister-in-law's protestations, Mr Eng decided to try out the geomancer's advice, at least on a temporary basis. The difference was astonishing. At the end of the first week, profits had mysteriously doubled, even though the number of orders remained the same. The girls all seemed much happier; and, strangest of all, even the quality of their work had improved enormously. He felt quite justified in giving everyone a bonus.

The only unhappy face was that of his sister-in-law. She seemed to be continually surly and angry. He wished he could do something to make her happier.

A week or so later, a delighted Mr Eng called Madam Lang to his office. With him were a prosperous-looking gentleman and a younger man whom she took, correctly, to be his son.

Mr Eng beamed. "Revered sister-in-law. I have such exciting news for you. You will be so happy." Madam Lang smiled politely, if somewhat apprehensively, at the strangers.

"This is Honourable Mr Teng and his respected son. There is such wonderful news, I scarcely know how to begin. However, firstly, as you know, our profits have been so improved since the *Feng Shui* expert came here . . . a wonderful man, Mr Teng, young, but so talented . . . that I have decided to employ the services of a clerk. Mr Teng's son will be joining us tomorrow. He will be able to take over many of the time-consuming tasks which trouble you at present."

Madam Lang's eyebrows rose momentarily.

"Secondly, Mr Teng has been so impressed with the samples of work from our factory, that he has decided to honour us with the commission of a huge wedding-banner, twelve feet in length."

Madam Lang attempted an enthusiastic smile. "Well, that is certainly very good news. Congratulations, brother-in-law."

Mr Eng clapped his hands. "No, no, dear sister-in-law. Congratulations are due to *you*. Mr Teng was so delighted with your excellent phoenix and dragon shawl, that he has insisted that you, yourself, embroider the banner.

"Oh dear, Cheng, bring some water, quickly! I'm afraid the dear lady has been quite overcome by the honour. And while you're about it, try to find out the cause of all that unseemly laughter in the workroom."

Many Westerners visiting the Far East have their first encounter with *Feng Shui* when they step off the Star Ferry on to Hong Kong Island, and see the Hong Kong and Shanghai Bank skyscraper towering up in front of them. It will not be long before someone points out the strangely-angled escalators which take visitors from the ground to the business floors. "That's because of the *Feng Shui*," an informant will tell them.

What else visitors might discover about *Feng Shui* will depend on the informant's depth of knowledge or experience. They may learn, for example, that many banks, restaurants, and other business buildings will call in a *Feng Shui* expert to advise on the siting of the entrance, as well as the official day of opening, though some proprietors may prefer to claim that they are merely considering the wishes of their staff, or clients.

Business buildings are designed to serve a variety of different purposes – manufacturing, accounting, and storage, for instance – but the principles which determine the *Feng Shui* of business premises are essentially the same as those applied to the home. The application of those principles is, however, directed towards different aims. A home needs a harmonious and stable atmosphere, providing a suitable environment for relaxation, self-improvement, comfort, nourishment, family welfare and sleep. These objectives are very different from those of the workplace, where the aim is to produce goods, or to provide a service for profit. Productive and energising *ch'i* are therefore required right through the industrial and commercial system, in order to stimulate enthusiasm, and the flow of trade. Relationships between all levels of management and staff need to be cordial, while the working conditions must be such that they are able to carry everyone through boring and repetitous tasks when necessary. And just as each room of the house would be approached in a slightly different way when assessing the suitability of the existing *Feng Shui*, so it is with industrial and commercial buildings: for what may appear to be unsuitable *Feng Shui* for one particular activity may well be ideal for another.

The employer who can identify the *ch'i* most suited to a certain type of work will be able to improve working conditions, thus reducing burdens on the staff, and increasing output. Employees, for their part, might also find that conditions can be improved by identifying deficiencies in the *Feng Shui* of their work-place. Certainly, nothing can be lost by trying to improve the working environment, since harmony and efficiency are closely related.

The first step is to distinguish each aspect of the work involved, as this will help to identify the type of *Feng Shui* to aim for. No matter how small the premises, it will be possible to isolate definite areas which belong to different stages of the work process.

Take a simple one-man shoe repair shop. In one corner stands the workbench: in another, all the materials needed for the repairs. On the other side are the shoes waiting for repair: and finally, separating customers from the happy confusion, is a well-worn wooden counter, over which the customer and cobbler discuss the nature of the repairs and prices. Thus, even in this tiny shop, it is possible to identify several distinct areas: the work-space; a corner for storage of materials; another for 'goods-in'; finished goods; and a counter for administration.

Work and change

Most work involves a process of change, even if only in location: apples from the tree to the stall of the fruiterer, coal from the ground, or fish from the sea, for instance. Alternatively, the form of something may be altered, just as the carpenter changes the form of wood to make a table, or an artist changes the appearance of paper. The material itself may also be modified, as when a foundryman converts red earth into white steel, or a baker processes flour into bread. Change may, however, be of a more intangible nature, too – as when a teacher processes ignorance to knowledge.

The title of China's most ancient book, the mystical work known as the *I Ching*, means, literally, the 'Book of Changes'. The Eight Trigrams, which form the foundation of this remarkable document, represent the various qualities associated with the eight stages in the transformation of *Yang* into *Yin*, and are symbolized by eight permutations of certain broken and unbroken lines. (The significance of the Eight Trigrams is explained more fully on pages 40-41.)

Each of the Eight Trigrams is associated with a particular quality and also a sphere of activity, as well as having its own associated compass direction. All forms of change can thus be summarized by the Eight Trigrams; and work will be performed more efficiently if the type of change taking place can be identified, and its surroundings and direction then determined according to the appropriate trigram.

So when a *Feng Shui* master is asked to help in the planning of the layout of a workshop, retail outlet, commercial enterprise, restaurant, or any other business activity, the nature of the work must first be assessed, and then its most appropriate trigram identified. Knowing the type of change involved in the activity points the geomancer to the appropriate trigram, and the trigram determines a suitable site for the particular work area.

The types of change associated with each of the Eight Trigrams, and consequently the ideal sphere of activity for each, are shown in the following chart.

Attracting custom

The function of the entrance to commercial premises is quite distinct from that of a house door. A home is a private affair, and the door is intended to welcome friends, and shut out intruders. The shop door, however, must not only welcome customers, it must positively attract them; while a bank needs to have solid-looking doors to inspire confidence and a sense of security.

Windows are another matter. House windows need to let in light and sunshine, permitting the occupants to look out on to the world, while also shutting out the prying gaze of the curious passer-by. Shop windows need to do the opposite, either revealing or hinting at the greatest possible variety of choice. Banks, however, may have no windows at all, suggesting that valuables deposited there are guarded safely.

If the entrance to commercial premises is to be designed so that the very best *Feng Shui* conditions are achieved, it is important, therefore, to consider the function of the building first. Buildings which are intended to attract custom need to have wide, spacious

The Eight Trigrams and Associated Activities

K'an NORTH

Danger, wheels, curves, flow
Suitable for workshops, race-tracks, and mechanical communication.

Ken NORTH-EAST

Barriers, non-movement
Suitable for entrances, security systems, porter's lodge, storage and warehousing.

Chen EAST

Movement, speed, roads
Suitable for depots, transport and distribution of goods generally.

Sun SOUTH-EAST

Continuous operation
Suitable for routine work, assembly lines, and typing-pools.

Li SOUTH

Fire, lightning
Suitable for processes using heat, electrical engineering, computers, or laboratories.

K'un SOUTH-WEST

Docility, nourishment
Suitable for medical centres, canteens, welfare, and agriculture.

Tui WEST

Reflections, joy
Suitable for recreation, theatres, restaurants, and other entertainment places.

Ch'ien NORTH-WEST

Strength, expansion, creativity
Suitable for management, design studios, and training premises.

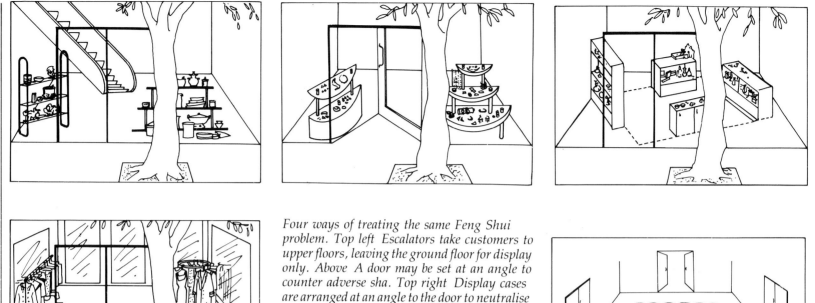

Four ways of treating the same Feng Shui problem. Top left Escalators take customers to upper floors, leaving the ground floor for display only. Above A door may be set at an angle to counter adverse sha. Top right Display cases are arranged at an angle to the door to neutralise poor Feng Shui. Left Mirrors are used to reflect adverse sha and to add a greater sense of space.

In places of entertainment, such as theatres, it is preferable to have doors opening outwards, to facilitate dispersal of exhausted ch'i.

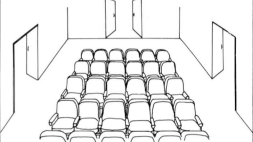

entrances; but because of this, they become more vulnerable to attack by unfavourable *sha*.

One of Hong Kong's few traditional-style shopping avenues, Nathan Road, is lined with trees along its more upmarket reaches. However, trees and pillars in front of windows and entrances are said to bring ill-fortune, and it is interesting to observe the various ways in which businesses have solved the resulting problem of adverse *sha*, at the same time adding to the effectiveness of the design of the premises. One large store takes all its customers to an upper level, using escalators arranged at a slanting angle and leaving the ground floor as a display area only. A narrow jewellers has the entrance door set at an angle – a popular method of countering adverse *sha* in commercial premises. A fashion shop effectively neutralises an adverse *Feng Shui* situation by putting all its shop fittings, display cases, and furnishings in a neat rectangle, set at an angle to the shop's frontage. Its neighbour lines the walls with mirrors, thereby adding brilliance to the interior, and giving the impression of greater space.

It is also most vital for businesses to stimulate beneficial *ch'i*, as well as deflecting harmful *sha*; and to this end, it is important to instal the right type of door. Fire regulations, however, often stipulate that exit doors in public buildings should open outwards. Fortunately, traditional *Feng Shui* principles need not conflict with legal requirements: and in cases where local legislation decrees that the premises must be provided with fire doors that open outwards, it is best for the flow of *ch'i* if these are available for emergencies only, rather than for general use. With fire doors in place, the main doors can then be inwardly-opening, two-way swing doors, or even sliding doors, which will permit an inward flow of *ch'i*.

Places of entertainment, such as cinemas, theatres and concert halls, however, have something in common with store-houses in that they are all generally windowless and, therefore, prone to build up stale air. Stagnant *ch'i* are regarded as harmful, and a potential danger to health. But closets, sheds, and pantries are, fortunately, invariably fitted with outwardly-opening doors which help to expel dead *ch'i* from the confined space. Consequently, in the case of non-residential public buildings of this type, it is actually preferable to have doors which open outwards as this effectively encourages the dispersal of exhausted *ch'i*.

The reception area

The very nature of any reception area is that it is the first point of contact for a visitor. The receptionist (that is, the person normally first encountered by the visitor) needs to be able to see the entrance; and, by the same token, the visitor also needs to see the receptionist.

However, *Feng Shui* principles demand that the reception desk must not be placed facing the door square on, as this acts as a barrier to good influences, even though it will also ward off malevolent ones. Rather, the ideal position for the receptionist is facing the door from a position shifted to one side. It would not be advisable, though, to have the receptionist placed in a side office, as this is not a welcoming position, nor one providing a good observation point. Chinese businesses, from the largest banks to the smallest offices, are also fond of installing rock and water gardens in the reception area, thereby providing stimulating *ch'i* and an aesthetically pleasing environment for visitor and employee alike.

Office premises

The head of a concern needs to be able to negotiate from a position of strength, and should be protected from any adverse *sha* which might affect important decision-making or planning. In this respect, the director or manager should occupy the *Feng Shui* position denoted by the trigram *Ch'ien* in order to administer successfully.

In ordinary circumstances, this will be found at the North-West position; but in commercial enterprises where the owner-director personally takes a very active role in the running of the company, it may be that the position of the director's office will have to be determined according to the personal horoscope, using a method as described on page 94.

The entrance door to the director's office should be in the long wall of a corridor, and not facing the length of the passageway, as this will expose the room to *sha* caused by the straight line. Furthermore, the door to the office should not be in the centre of the wall facing the director, as this could expose the occupant to danger

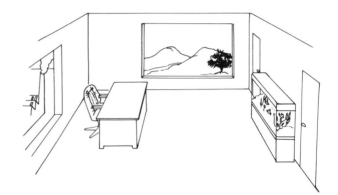

In many respects, this may seem to be the ideal director's office: but, in fact, from a Feng Shui point-of-view, the desk should have its back to a wall and not a window. Ideally, too, there should be two windows – one with a view of the factory, and the other of the surrounding landscape.

immediately the door is opened. Rather, the entrance door should be to one side, close to a wall, and perhaps balanced by a second door in the same wall, which might lead to a secretary's office, or to other rooms in the director's suite.

The director's desk should have its back to a wall, with a window to one side. Windows facing the desk should be avoided, as these cause glare, nor should a window be behind the desk, as this puts the director into silhouette, thereby weakening the impression registered by visitors.

Ideally, there will be two windows, but these should

not be facing. From one window there should be a prime view of the surroundings which give the site its ideal *Feng Shui* location; while from the other, the director should be able to cast a supervisory eye and observe the comings and goings of everyday commercial activity. Should it happen, however, that unfavourable *Feng Shui* is generated by the functional shapes of buildings outside, the inauspicious Element should be identified from its shape and rendered ineffective by the careful positioning of appropriate items in the office itself, as in the example given on pages 92-93.

In a business environment, too, rather different *Feng Shui* criteria apply to the arrangement and positioning of furniture. At home, a good host will endeavour to put guests on an equal level: but the placing of the chairs in the director's office may deliberately aim to put the visitor at disadvantage. Even if the director takes an expansive attitude, and moves in front of the desk in order to appear to be on equal footing with the visitor, a dominant position can be maintained if the visitor is placed with the back to the door or window, and therefore in a situation vulnerable to *sha*.

Secretarial services

For convenience, the secretary or personal assistant's office will probably be adjacent to the director's office. It is, in fact, highly desirable for the secretary's office to be placed so that the creative *ch'i*, coming from the directors office, flow into it. The door from the director's room should open into the secretary's office; and the secretary's desk should be sideways to the window, preferably with the secretary's back to the wall, so that the desk faces but is not directly opposite the door.

The open-plan office

Unfortunately, it is a fact of business life that much of the work performed by clerical staff is of a routine nature. Management is therefore obliged to see that the situation is made as happy as possible in order to compensate for the tedium of such processes.

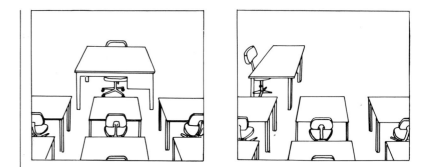

In an open-plan office, a great deal of work may be fairly routine. To alleviate boredom and encourage harmony, Feng Shui demands that desks are not arranged as in a classroom, but with the supervisor seated at an angle to the rest of the staff.

While it may be convenient to arrange desks in neat rows in typing pools and other offices where large numbers of personnel are involved in routine work, according to *Feng Shui* principles it is unwise to have the supervisor at a facing desk, classroom-fashion, as this is intimidating to staff and may create a potential source of conflict. A much more harmonious atmosphere can be sustained if the supervisor is seated at an angle to the clerical staff, promoting a greater feeling of team effort.

Efficiency can be further stimulated by judicious use of colour. Routine work is symbolized by the Element Earth, produced by the Element Fire. Thus, by introducing into the environment occasional splashes of bright colour, especially red – fresh flowers or cheerful posters, for instance – the performance of routine tasks will be made less onerous.

Work within drawing offices and design studios, is basically creative, no matter how routine. The prevailing Element of creative processes is Wood. The Element which produces Wood is Water, and so this should be in evidence, either decoratively, such as in an aquarium, or functionally, as in a drinking fountain.

According to some *Feng Shui* authorities, in environments which involve considerable reliance on electronic devices, cables and other apparatus should be placed along the path followed by the natural *ch'i*, instead of being arranged haphazardly around the room.

The factory

Whether a factory is attached to a company's offices or located on another site altogether, its position is likely to be determined by very practical considerations, such as proximity to railways, waterways, or other transport facilities. It may also be necessary to have access to a source of raw materials, power, and a facility for the disposal of waste. Once all such practicalities have been considered, the lay-out of the factory can all be planned according to *Feng Shui* principles.

In the factory, too, if the trigram associated with a particular location is also appropriate for the work process taking place there, then – according to the doctrines of *Feng Shui* – Heaven and Earth are in harmony, resulting in benefit for those who are under their twin influences. Work is not always enjoyable, but it can be made less of a drudge if the *Feng Shui* conditions are favourable, the environment made more stimulating, and the chore of everyday labour thereby lessened.

First of all, once again every effort should be made to identify the specific stages of the work process, so that these can be assigned to the area in accordance with the appropriate trigram. The machine shop, for example, with its lathes and wheels, will be best situated to the direction *K'an*, trigram VI, North; the assembly line, representing routine work, should be placed towards the direction *Sun*, trigram II, South-East, as this represents continuous operation. Furnace or foundry work, or even a bakery,

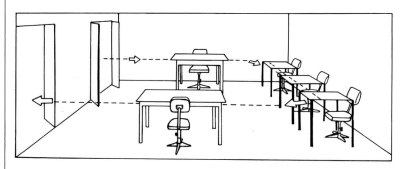

In a light industrial unit, work stations should ideally follow the flow of the ch'i, with the entrance in the North-West and goods exit at the South-West position.

will be most favourably placed in the direction *Li*, trigram III, South.

In a small, light industrial factory, work stations should follow the flow of the *ch'i*. Ideally, the entrance to the workshop or assembly area should be from the North-West, represented by the first trigram, *Ch'ien*; and finished products should be taken away through the South-West, symbolized by the trigram *K'un*.

Heavy industrial processes are more suited to a scheme where the *ch'i* are encouraged to flow along a North-South alignment. In addition, water-pipes, gas mains, electric cables and drainage should follow the production route. In brief, the planning and design of the

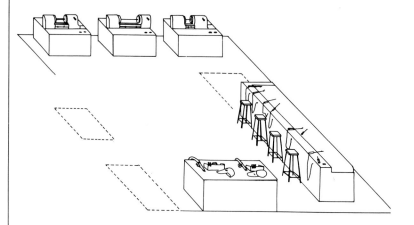

In heavy industrial premises, Feng Shui principles declare that ch'i should flow North-South, and that cables and drainage follow the production line, without crossing over at all – thereby also making maintenance very much more simple.

services should be as simple as possible. Not only is it considered poor *Feng Shui* for service pipes, cables and mains supplies to cross over each other, it also makes sound practical sense for such services to be easily accessible, for maintenance purposes.

The ideal shapes for architectural features or internal fittings can also be determined by *Feng Shui* principles: and as the manufacturing process is concerned with production, a shape associated with the Element *producing* the Element most pertinent to the manufacturing process will be the ideal one to feature. For example, if the manufacturing process involves fire, the ideal shape to stimulate production would be a long tube, column, or cylinder, since this shape is associated with the controlling Element, Wood, which – as shown in the chart on page 89 – produces Fire.

For wet processes – such as dyeing, or the chemical treatments of goods – the ideal Element to feature is Metal, as this produces Water. Metal is represented by rounded shapes, and the colour white. In this sort of factory, dark corners should therefore be avoided by using as much light paintwork as possible. Attention to such *Feng Shui* principles will also improve visibility and safety on site.

Processes involving change of shape or form involve creativity, and therefore pertain to the Element Wood, produced by Water. The availability of ample supplies of fresh water will assist in keeping down dust, also providing refreshment for the work-force.

No matter how eminently practical the industrial process may seem, consideration of the principles of *Feng Shui* will nearly always enhance the quality of the working environment for personnel, and thereby add to greater efficiency.

Shops and stores

For centuries, *Feng Shui* practitioners have been advising clients on how best to plan retail premises in order to ensure maximum sales success. Although the disposition of goods on display, the location of those still in storage, and even the position of the cash register are vital factors which have to be taken into consideration, they all take second place to the nature of the shop's entrance which should actively funnel beneficial *ch'i* into the shop. A wide-mouthed doorway, so it is said, will help to catch both the customer and the flow of *ch'i*. In order to counteract poor *Feng Shui*, doors are sometimes positioned at a slant, and have the additional merit of providing a limited area of standing room within the boundaries of the shop. Psychologically, this little triangle

between the frontage of the shop and the street acts as a kind of threshold, the customer feeling encouraged to make the effort to enter the shop.

The rule that stairs and corridors in the home should not face doors applies equally where business premises are concerned. But, if this occurs, and it is impractical to alter the internal structure, then the arrangement of displays of goods should be such that the customer is obliged to make a change in direction on entering the shop. If the customer has to change direction, it can be assumed that the *ch'i* will change direction, too, with beneficial results.

Another effective way to divert *ch'i* is to line the walls with mirrors. These will not only display goods to potential customers at all manner of angles, but will also increase the brightness of the shop, providing a more stimulating environment for commerce. (This works well in business premises, but would be unsuitable for a family residence, since the energizing *ch'i* produced would soon burn up a harmonious atmosphere within the home.)

Feng Shui identifies two categories of sales-outlet: 'open', where goods may be readily handled, and 'closed', where items are presented for inspection on request.

In an 'open' shop – such as a greengrocer's – the owner may feel that it is best to have the cash register near the exit, in order to deter thieves from leaving the shop with goods which have not been paid for. But some Chinese geomancers maintain that the ideal situation for the cash register is one which harmonizes with the horoscope of the owner. On page 96, you will find an example explaining how such a calculation can be made, with the aid of the Western version of the *Lo P'an*. Where there is no single owner, however, the position of the cash register is most suited to the South-East.

When planning the interior of a shop, the cash-point, display, and entrance should be considered in turn. If the shop is of the 'open' type, the object is firstly to encourage as many customers as possible into the shopping area; secondly, for them to be able to examine the goods; and thirdly, to buy. Thus, consideration of the entrance comes first; display of the goods, second; and finally, the cash-point. Ideally, the entrance should be

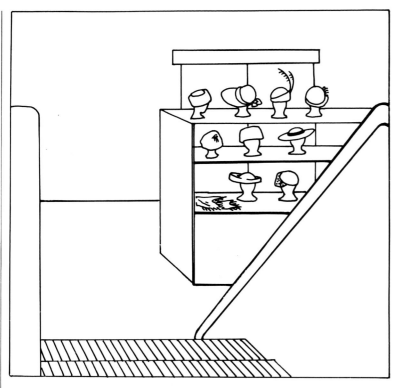

In business premises, too, stairs should not face doors. Wherever this occurs, however, a display of goods, judiciously placed, will remedy the adverse Feng Shui by altering the flow of the ch'i.

placed in the South-West (the receiving direction); but if this is not possible, certain compensatory arrangements can be made by means of interior lay-out, so that customers proceed towards the South-West on entering. Alternatively, large mirrors should be placed in the South-West to reflect the entrance. Supermarkets, despite their size, are a good example of the 'open' shop.

In the 'closed' type of shop, such as a jeweller's premises, however, security of the stock is the most important consideration and its placing therefore has to be worked out first; the position of entrance, second; and the cash-point, third. A geomancer would thus recommend that the display of stock is placed in the North-East, since this represents safe-keeping.

In an agency establishment – such as insurance or real estate brokers – the administration of funds is the first concern; the entrance, the second; and the display of goods, probably negligible. It follows that such businesses are best suited to premises which have a North-West to South-East axis, since these directions are associated with management and trade. But whatever the orientation of the premises, if the furnishings can be arranged to encourage general movement along these axes, according to *Feng Shui* theory, this will encourage the development of a thriving business.

Feng Shui principles also dictate that predominant shapes and colours should be based on the Element associated with the type of merchandise or service which is being offered. Groceries, greengrocery, and books and magazines, for instance, belong to the Element Wood, which suggests cylindrical and tubular forms, as well as blues and greens. Chemical products, and electrical goods and services, belong to the Element Fire, represented by sharp-cornered designs, and the colour red. Pottery and builders' materials belong to the Element Earth, represented by square shapes, and yellow or brown hues. The Element Metal covers metalware and jewellery, and is represented by round shapes, metallic colours, and white; while wine and spirit merchants, petrol stations and agency services are ruled by the Element Water, represented by irregular shapes and black or very dark shades. Thus, the nature of the shop or store should come prominently to the fore when considering matters of interior design.

Commerce and trade are subject to many whims and changes. For centuries, the Chinese have believed that, though the rises and falls of fortune may not be totally harnessed, they can at least be guided. Thus, while orientation may seem at first to have little to do with manufacture or sales, if the forces of Heaven and Earth can be made to complement each other, then harmony, success, and prosperity will be the consequence.

PART FIVE
The Garden

*How the Perfect Prospect
inspires Tranquillity*

Mei Li tried to fight back her tears. She clenched her hands, and beat them together fiercely. "But Nana, I know I love him more than my elder sister does. Why can't it be me he's marrying?" Revered Grandmother took the girl's hand, and followed Mei Li's younger brother across the stepping stones. "You mustn't fret, little granddaughter. This is something you just have to accept as part of life. The contract was entered into by our families many years ago. Who knows? Perhaps Eldest Daughter Hsiang really does love him. Be brave, Mei Li, and forget the young marquis."

"How will I ever forget him, when my love is so strong?"

"To tell you truly, Mei Li, I don't think you are in love."

"Oh, Nana, that's not true. I know I love him. I can feel it so strongly."

"I think love is stronger than your feelings are now, little granddaughter. Why, if you were really in love, you would be so light of heart that you could walk on driven snow and not leave a footprint. Is that how you feel?"

Mei Li shook her head. "No, Nana, not like that."

"Then I think what you are suffering from is jealousy, and not love."

"Love!" laughed Youngest Son Pei Ling. "That's all girls ever think about! Come on, we've got to compose some more titles for the garden views to please the wedding guests. I've done all the work so far. Isn't it time you thought up a few lines of your own?"

"Perhaps your brother is right," said Mei Li's grandmother, gently. "To work, then. What title shall we paste up here, by the pond?"

They stepped into the viewing pavilion; and Mei Li, with a sigh, looked over the bridge into the water. Without enthusiasm, she replied: "Oh well, then. What about: *Seeing my reflection in the water*?

Nana laughed. "Not very inspiring, is it? Let me see what we can do to improve it. The Water Element's direction is North, and its colour is black. So why not say: *That cool, dark, pool has captured my reflection*?"

Mei Li managed to smile. "Nana, you *are* clever."

Pei Ling quickly painted a few characters on a red piece of paper, and pasted it on one of the pillars of the pavilion. "Now to the next spot," he urged.

They made their way to the next viewing area – a moon gate, from which could be seen five willow trees, their branches woven together like a curtain. Revered Grandmother had just begun to explain that each of the trees represented one of the Five Elements, so forming a picture of peace and harmony, when suddenly Pei Ling motioned everyone to be still. A few yards in front of them, a kestrel was hovering; but soon, becoming aware of their presence, it flew off.

"How beautiful it was!" gasped Mei Li.

Nana nodded. "That certainly merits a line, doesn't it? What can we use?"

"*Caught unawares, a hovering kestrel*," suggested Pei Ling, with enthusiasm.

"No, that's too obvious," said Mei Li thoughtfully. "The titles should be like riddles, and make the guests ponder." Mei Li suddenly became sadly thoughtful about the reason that would bring the guests there.

"My riddle will be: *Still it is, though beating*," she said.

Pei Ling shook his head doubtfully, but wrote out the sign and fixed it to a tree.

The three continued their journey round the garden, Revered Grandmother stopping them at suitable vantage points to admire the views, and also the forms and shapes which could be best observed from a particular spot. Now and then, she would ask Mei Li to compose a line, and Pei Ling to paint it in his excellent calligraphy.

The stroll round the gardens had lifted Mei Li's spirits a little, but Pei Ling was beginning to get bored, and wanted to get back to the house. Finally, they came to the temporary ceremonial gate, erected to celebrate the wedding of Mei Li's elder sister.

"Well, this is where the guests will take their leave tomorrow. What do you think we should write here?"

"What about: *Meeting friends from afar. Is not that delightful?*" suggested Pei Ling.

Revered Grandmother frowned. "It's always good to have a quotation from the sage Confucius, but that text would be more appropriate, I think, for a greeting than for a departure."

Pei Ling kicked a stone. "Let's go home" he said abruptly. "It's beginning to get dark."

"Why, that's a suitable subject for a line," said Nana. "*The sun goes down, but rises again the next day*. What do you think, Mei Li?"

Mei Li considered it for a moment, and offered: "*I leave tonight, but tomorrow I return*."

"Delightful," said Nana. "But look how dark it is getting. We must return, too. I think we'll have to take a short cut along the avoidance lane, and then through the azalea grove."

The three hurried on towards the house, with only a minor mishap as they skirted the pond: amid much laughter, Mei Li nearly lost her right shoe, as she trod through the mud.

Nana pointed at the thick black footprints Mei Li had left behind. "Look there," she laughed. "You can't say you are in love, leaving footprints like those."

The wedding passed. Hsiang was married to her handsome marquis, and Mei Li was learning to survive with her infatuation.

One day, some weeks later, the family were escorting a few guests round the garden. The party sauntered happily, admiring and commenting on the views and the exotic plants and fountains that had attracted attention as a result of Pei Ling's riddles. As they were crossing the stepping stones of the carp pool, Mei Li noticed one of the guests, a stranger to her, looking at her intently. It made her feel confused. As soon as she thought his attention was elsewhere, she tried to get a better look at him, but he suddenly turned, and caught her glance.

When they reached the pond, Nana told the guests that Mei Li had written the title to that view.

"Indeed?" said the stranger. "Please allow me to read it. *That cool, dark, pool has captured my reflection,*" he recited, and then looked straight into Mei Li's eyes.

There was a murmur of approval from the guests. Mei Li hid her face in her sleeve.

As they continued their stroll, Nana took Mei Li by the arm. Quite casually, and seemingly without referring to anyone in particular, she said: "His name is Wei Tzu, cousin to the marquis."

Soon, they came to the moon gate where Pei Ling had seen the kestrel. The guests clustered round the inscription, and Mei Li found Wei Tzu standing next to her. Very softly, almost as if he wanted no one but Mei Li to hear, he read: "*Still it is, though beating.* Now what in such a lovely garden could be still, but beating? It would have to be something exceptionally beautiful."

Landscapes in Miniature

Miniature gardens, known as *bonsai* (from the Chinese *Pen-tsai*, meaning 'bowl cultivation'), originated in Su-chou. There, regional architecture took the form of a series of buildings which grew round a central courtyard. The sun paid only a fleeting visit to each spot, and the custom arose of making portable plant-pot gardens which could be moved round the courtyard to catch its rays. In time, dwarf plants were cultivated to stand beside delicately veined rocks, leading to the exquisite miniature landscapes we know today.

The miniature landscape garden has the great advantage of revealing the great through the small, and is created to be viewed from particular angles.

For full appreciation, this should be in solitude.

In order to create a miniature landscape, there are just three essentials: a plant, a pot, and a rock: and, again, these should not be exceeded, or the landscape will be incongruous.

Such miniature landscapes may be constructed either for contemplation out-of-doors, in a small yard, or they may be intended as indoor gardens. Western indoor adaptions often use tropical or desert plants which are slow-growing and can cope with an indoor climate. Outdoor bonsai gardens will incorporate plants of the region. In China, they are shown to their best effect when displayed in tiny courtyards, against white-painted walls.

The guests made several fruitless attempts to solve the riddle, and then called on Mei Li to reveal the answer. She found herself strangely tongue-tied, however, and Nana had to tell them: "Why, the line refers to a hovering kestrel that was here."

Soon, all too soon, the guests arrived at the Western gate, framing the setting sun. They had already made their way through the crowded gateway, and Mei Li found herself standing alone. She looked over towards the young man, with whom she had not shared a single word directly, and found herself wondering if their families would ever meet again. Suddenly, Wei Tzu called out: "Wait, I haven't yet read the last inscription."

He took down the paper, and said: "This is an easy riddle: *I leave tonight, but tomorrow I return.*"

"Why, it means the sun!" cried the guests, pleased that they had guessed so quickly.

Looking at Mei Li, Wei Tzu said, "But often these riddles have hidden meanings, known only to one or two people. Who knows that this isn't such a riddle?"

The guests made their farewells, and began the journey homewards.

Mei Li made her own way back to the house, feeling strangely elated, and filled with a sensation she had never experienced before. She came to the path between the carp pond and the azaleas. This time, to save her shoes, she pulled them off, and skipped over the mud, barefooted. A carp leapt up at a fly, breaking the surface of the calm pool. Hearing the splash, Mei Li turned, and noticed something very remarkable. Of course, it may have been the effect of the ripples. But it was curious, nevertheless. For where she had just stepped through the mud at the water's edge, there was not a footprint to be seen.

When designing a garden, the Chinese have the very opposite of Western objectives. Thus the *Feng Shui* garden has no formal flower beds, nor neat rows of regulated blooms, nor riots of colour. Instead, it meticulously attempts to recreate the very best features of Nature, and to become a slice of the landscape, or even a landscape in miniature. The true secret of Chinese gardening is to create space in order to draw attention to detail. In doing this, the Chinese gardener may well take away where the Western gardener would add. Tiny gardens may be made even smaller by partitions; walls may be built to shut out features which are not part of the design; and a single plant may stand for many plants, as a perfect *Feng Shui* location is created in miniature, the principal costs being time, hard work, and patience. The garden can also include features which reveal the Dragon, the Bird, the Tiger and the Tortoise. Malevolent *sha* will be fended off by a token trellis; while a simply constructed pond may function as the garden's own Water Dragon. Thus, in attention to the shapes of walls, paths, rocks, and water, gardens can become model examples of all the precepts of the Form school of *Feng Shui*.

Shaped by Heaven

There are actually no firm rules and no fixed formulae for creating the perfect Chinese garden; only a number of basic principles. The first of these must be that qualities matter more than size; more, too, than the quantity, rarity, or variety of flowers. A single, common, wild plant, carefully placed, in an appropriate setting, will be worthy of contemplation; an over-crowded plot, on the other hand, will not attract a second glance: and if the garden is small, then the more sparsely it is laid out, the more spacious it will seem.

The second principle is that, before work on the garden begins, an overall design should be drawn up and maintained. It may take many years before the design is realised, and there may be great temptations to depart from the original plan: but unless these are resisted, the garden will be formless.

Thirdly, and all-importantly, the garden should reflect Nature. It may have been constructed by Man, but it should appear as if shaped by Heaven. It should be beautiful without being gaudy. The tones should be light, yet full of meaning; and there should be a balance between excess and emptiness, while strength is to be contrasted with gentleness. The garden must also have certain highlights, so that a visitor's eye is easily drawn to particular features, rather than baffled by a whole array of sights. Indeed, it is very much the garden designer's task to separate that which is beautiful from that which is ugly.

Static and mobile gardens

There are two kinds of Chinese garden: the 'static' and the 'mobile'. The 'static' garden is designed to be viewed as a whole, usually from one particular vantage point, where the composition can be seen at its best. The 'mobile' garden, however, is designed to be viewed piece by piece by the passer-by. The 'static' garden is thus much like a framed painting on the wall, seen all at once; while the 'mobile' garden is like a scroll painting, unfurled scene by scene. All well-planned gardens belong to one or other category, and some may even combine both functions. A badly thought-out garden, however, achieves neither.

The first step in designing a garden according to *Feng Shui* principles is to consider its function. Is it to be a 'static' garden, to be viewed from a window, perhaps; or is it to be a 'mobile' garden, through which the observer wanders, noting its different features in turn? A 'mobile' garden may have several enchanting miniature scenes, yet may not look particularly attractive when viewed from a distant window. The 'static' garden, however, may present a handsome appearance from a distance, but be less rewarding for the visitor who likes to take a stroll.

The 'static' garden is designed to be viewed from a particular vantage point, much like a framed painting. The 'mobile' garden, however, is more like a scroll painting, gradually unfurling its various features for the observer taking a stroll.

Space and perspective

Many Chinese gardens have smaller gardens within them. Yet in one respect, every Chinese garden is one garden inside another, for the surrounding landscape is viewed as part of the garden, and should be incorporated into it skilfully by using distant views to add to the appreciation of space and perspective.

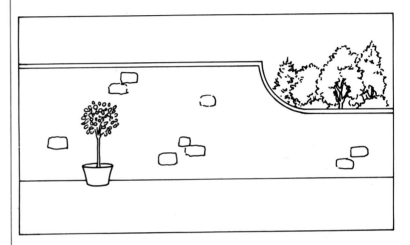

Feng Shui precepts declare that the tops of natural features in distant scenery may be seen from a garden, but not their bases; while in an industrial landscape, even an unattractive feature can be framed by a moon gate to lend perspective to the view.

The Chinese hold that some aspect of distant scenery should always be preserved and utilised, and this is usually achieved by 'taking away' any unrequired part by screening it with structured walls, a trellis, or trees. Only the tops of distant hills or mountains should be seen, and their bases should be hidden. Similarly, if the prospect is man-made, show the roofs, but not the bases. Even if the landscape is an industrial one, without a single natural feature, it should still be possible to identify its most attractive element and to isolate this from the rest. A chimney, framed in a moon gate, for instance, will add an intriguing degree of perspective to even the tiniest town garden.

Flower-Arranging

Like *bonsai*, the Chinese art of flower placement (*Ch'a Hua*) came to the Western world by way of Japan. Its origins and development are due to Buddhism, which encouraged the practice of making floral offerings to Heaven, to replace the animal sacrifices of earlier, less enlightened times. Subsequently, the presentation of flowers in the temple developed into an art which migrated to the household altar; and it eventually gave rise to the highly organised art form known as *ikebana*.

The main difference between Western and Oriental methods of flower-arranging is the extreme economy of material found in Eastern displays, which often comprise merely a twig or two, with remarkably few flowers and just a hint of foliage.

Pots used in *ikebana* fall into two distinct classes – the upright or vase-type, and the horizontal or bowl-type – the nature of container dictating the kind of arrangement which can be made. The upright vase lends itself to arrangements which cascade to the base, moving to the Earth; while the bowl-type suggests arrangements which reach upwards, moving towards Heaven. Whatever type of arrangement is made, the bowl or vase is never obscured but is always regarded as part of the ensemble. Low, flat bowls suggest water, and often a large flat dish will be used for an arrangement which occupies only a fraction of the surface, leaving an expanse of level water as an integral part of the arrangement.

The apparently sparing use of flowers, branches and foliage may belie the almost extravagant length to which material is rejected. Given a bunch of roses, for example, the oriental flower-arranger is likely to select only one bloom, chosen for the angle at which it falls, or the depth of colour, or fullness of flower. In oriental arranging, it is not what is used which is the criterion, but what is *not* used. In composing an arrangement, it is better to take away, than to add.

Choice of plants

The very best plants to have in a garden, according to Chinese *Feng Shui* tradition, are those which might have found their way into it naturally. The garden should serve to bring out the beauty of local plants, rather than include something which is alien to that region. In essence, the *Feng Shui* garden is not concerned with exotic flora, foreign to the natural landscape, and therefore incongruous: nor is it intended to be a collection of botanical specimens.

Trees usually form the background to a Chinese garden, and are often used to screen rejected scenery. In general, evergreens are preferable to deciduous trees, and are seen as symbols of longevity. Willows are a great favourite of garden designers, in both the East and the West. But the Chinese regard willows as suitable only for large gardens, since they consider these trees only to be effective when they appear in groups of three or five. The effect sought is that of a heavy curtain, rather than the gentle droop of a single willow, as often encountered in the large Western garden.

Willows are greatly admired by Chinese garden designers, but usually planted in groups of three or five to form a heavy curtain, rather than singly. They are therefore mostly found in larger gardens.

Use of colour

The Chinese garden does not have to be a rainbow of colour. Indeed, the gaudiness of blazing contrasts is thought to disturb both the garden's appearance and its *Feng Shui*. Instead, the finest Chinese gardens keep to a discriminating, narrow spectrum. Yet it would need all the colours of the palette to paint the rich variety of shades to be seen. The colours of autumn might serve as a model. Thought they are seemingly all golds and browns, blending perfectly, the number of hues is endless.

White is not a colour, and water is certainly colourless in itself. Yet they both serve to enhance and reflect the colours of their surroundings in the traditional Chinese garden. In Northern China, the blue-green of the pines and the blue of the frosty sky are magnified when crisp white clouds drift across; while in Southern China, pavilions with white-washed walls, leaning over water, may seem to have no colour, yet every colour.

The gardener, alert to the principles of *Feng Shui*, will also endeavour to keep to regional hues which come from the colour of the local earth, rocks, sand and natural vegetation, and will use these natural shades to greater aesthetic advantage than the one who tries to hide them with showy displays of transient colour.

Wet and dry rockeries

Every Chinese garden features rocks, comprising either a few carefully arranged stones, or a veritable grotto. In Western gardens, rockeries are constructed principally to support a few alpine plants; but in China, the rocks are there to be admired for their own form. One of the most famous rock-gardens recorded is that of the Hui-tsung Emperor. When he ascended the throne in 1100 AD, he had no sons, a state of affairs which *Feng Shui* advisers attributed to the flatness of the terrain. As a result, he ordered a mountain be built to the North-East of the capital. Hundreds of cart-loads of huge rocks, worn by water into fantastic shapes, were brought from Lake T'ai near Su-chou, China's Garden City. The Emperor had his sons; but due to the extravagance of building the mountain, he was to lose his empire.

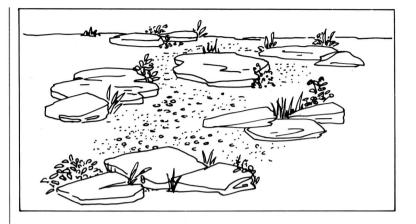

*To achieve balance, rugged (Yang) rocks are placed within the flat (Yin)
setting of a 'dry' rockery.*

How a rockery is designed will depend on whether it is planned to be 'dry' or 'wet'. 'Wet' rockeries do not necessarily involve water, however, since the very formation of the rocks can create an illusion of the presence of water. Scattered rocks belong to the 'dry' type of rockery. A good piece of rockery will look natural and integrated, rather than built or assembled: and the types of rocks used need to be considered in relation to each other. Delicate rocks lend a feminine touch; rugged ones, a masculine one: and the aim should be to balance the *Yin* and *Yang* of the garden by placing rugged (*Yang*) rocks in a flat (*Yin*) setting, and vice versa. In Southern China, the silhouettes of rocks are often highlighted by bright sunshine and the background of a white-washed wall, forming a sharp and compact composition.

Ponds and streams

A Chinese garden is not complete without water; and the nature of the ground will always determine how it should be incorporated. If flat, it will be in the form of ponds; if hilly, with streamlets: and in either case, it is not the depth of the water which is important, but its surface appearance, shape and sinuosity. Clearly, too, in 'wet' areas, it will be important to attend to the drainage of the water, so that floods do not occur; while in 'dry' areas, greater attention must be paid to preserving the water.

Water is also valued for the contribution it makes to the 'sound picture' in a garden: the gurglings of streams, and the splashing of carp in ponds are all part of the total piece of Nature captured in a Chinese garden landscape. Chinese ornamental gardens with very large ponds also frequently have ornamental paths or bridges, built above the surface of the water, and leading to island pavilions. To counteract any baleful *sha*, these bridges are always made in a zig-zag pattern, the theorists asserting that there should always be nine 'curves' or bends. Sometimes, too, such garden bridges are constructed close to the surface of the pond, and lower than the tops of the banks, as this creates the wonderful sensation of stepping on the very surface of the water.

Features and follies

All types of Chinese garden may incorporate features which are neither plants nor rocks, but man-made. In the largest gardens, these may take the form of many-storeyed pagodas, pavilions, and tea-houses. It is also common for miniature (bonsai) gardens to incorporate tiny models of architectural features: but a more modest garden should not include representations of grander objects. Rather, it is thought preferable to feature something in proportion to the size of the garden, such as a sundial, armillary sphere, or pergola.

If there is a garden shed or other utility, ideally this should either become a feature of the garden, or else be completely hidden. On no account should an attempt be made to fancify it with touches such as lattice windows, forming it into a pseudo-temple or tea-house.

Walls, however, can be used in many ways to enhance the features of a garden: and suitably placed in small gardens, they can actually give the illusion of greater space, by adding to the number of angles and views. Indeed, the Chinese say that walls should be used to conceal what should be concealed, screen what should be screened, separate what should be separated, and divide what should be divided.

Winding and straight paths

In 'mobile' gardens, there will be winding paths to take the visitor to the various vantage points. Such paths become a feature of the garden. On the other hand, short cuts, for convenience, need to be concealed, as they take the form of unnatural straight lines. These were known to the Chinese as 'avoidance lanes', originally intended for servants, to enable them to fetch and carry from the main mansion without having to encounter guests on the way. Sinuous paths, like streams, are the most favoured; but tradition demands that spirals "like a poisonous snake wound round the neck" (*On Chinese Gardens*, Chen Cong Zhou, 1984) should be completely avoided.

Naming the site

One of the ways in which Chinese teachers of landscape painting get their students to develop an appreciation of scenic formations is to encourage them to compose descriptive titles for different aspects of the landscape in front of them. This also helps the eye to capture detail. Thus, in Kuei-lin (the home of the Form or scenic school of *Feng Shui*, and a magnet for Chinese painters for more than a thousand years), all kinds of imaginative names have been given to aspects of the local scenery. 'Piled Brocades', 'Crescent Moon', 'Fishing Crane', 'Golden Carp' and, most famous of all, 'Elephant Hill', are just a few of the hundreds of titles bestowed on various features of the landscape over the centuries.

Just as names were given to the scenery, tradition holds, too, that titles are given to views in the private garden. Indeed, no good *Feng Shui* site should be without a name. The celebrated Ming Dynasty novel, *A Dream of Red Mansions* by Ts'ao Hsüeh-ch'in and Kao O, states: "If no inscriptions on tablets are made for the pavilions and halls in a garden with such splendid views, then flowers, windows, hills and ponds will all fail to add their colours." But this custom was ancient even then. Many centuries before, the great eighth-century poet Tu Fu had written the lines: "Leaning forward to dip my brush into the inkstone on the balustrade, I set down poems on the Chinese parasol leaves before me". In fact, some Chinese teachers went so far as to declare that only when a title was given to the scenery would its true splendour be unveiled. A casual passer-by, it was believed, might never notice those finer features which an imaginative title would identify.

Another delightful custom, in some oriental gardens, is the practice of pasting up mottoes or quotations at various points, their hidden meanings often used to convey secret messages between lovers. Traditionally, at night, inscriptions in the form of riddles would be written on paper lanterns, and a stroll round the garden would thus be combined with a form of entertainment for the family and guests.

Positive qualities

When choosing a name for a site, *Feng Shui* principles dictate that you should always stress the positive and actual. For instance, a name like 'Dragon Searching for Riches' would be considered unlucky, because it implies that riches had still not been found. But 'Dragon Finding Treasure' or 'Dragon Vomiting Jewels' suggest the accumulation of wealth – although the last example unfortunately loses something in translation.

The scenery need not be breath-taking; in fact, the less inspiring the terrain, the greater the imagination needs to stretch itself. There is always some aspect that can be singled out to receive a favourable, positive-sounding title. The local reservoir takes on a new significance when given the name 'Jade Turtle Pool'; while even the unrelieved silhouette of a clothing factory might be more auspiciously called 'Gold Canopy over Tiger Weaving Brocade'.

Whether for *Feng Shui*, landscape appreciation, or merely for private enjoyment, studying features of the skyline and inventing poetic names for otherwise all-too-familiar situations is to be thoroughly recommended as a pleasant and rewarding exercise.

PART SIX

The Lo P'an

*How Perfect Concordance
establishes Serenity*

The two children scampered gleefully down the old corridors, throwing up clouds of dust behind them. Po, their older brother, watched happily. But on turning round to his parents, his smile suddenly faded, for it seemed that his mother had been crying. His father was speaking to her reassuringly. This wonderful mansion belonged to them, now. So, Po wondered, what could possibly be wrong?

"Don't blame yourself, Liu Hua. You couldn't have known that it would be like this, even though the notary did warn us that the mansion had seen better days."

"But we didn't expect a ruin. Oh, Chen, what made me persuade you to come here – to this?"

Her husband smiled ruefully. "You know I didn't need any persuasion."

The truth was that, when the letter had arrived, (addressed, much to their amusement, to the *Lady* Wu), Chen's first reaction was to resign from his employment: and, somewhat rashly, he had couched the letter of resignation in such terms that his departure was both immediate and irrevocable. The death of his wife's great-uncle, someone she had never met, meant that Liu Hua had inherited a mansion, title and estate in a distant province. When the news first broke, it promised romance and excitement. Now, in the cold Northern light, the reality was quite a different matter.

The old notary climbed the steps towards them. "Not as comfortable as Shanghai" he called, more as a statement than a question. "I told you the mansion had seen better days. Your great-uncle thought he was the last of the line. I don't think that he even realised you existed, my Lady. It took some trouble to trace you. I hope you think it was worth it."

"Indeed, it was, Sir" said Chen, before his wife could even begin to answer.

"Well, may it bring you better luck than all its previous occupants. According to legend, no one will be happy in this house until its rightful owners have taken possession, and the ancestral gate is restored."

"But aren't *we* the rightful owners?" asked Liu Hua.

"Legally, yes. But with all respect, my Lady," said the old man, wiping his forehead, "many people would claim that the Wu family never owned this mansion by right. Centuries ago, it is said to have belonged to the Lord of Sui, reputedly one of the richest men in the whole of China. Naturally, he had his enemies; and a certain General Wu, your honourable great-uncle's revered ancestor, plotted to gain the fortune for himself. He had the Lord of Sui accused of treason on some trumped-up charge, and banished. As a reward for this loyalty, or rather treachery, the Emperor then awarded the estate and fortune to General Wu. But the crafty Lord of Sui must have managed to escape with his fortune, for there was nothing of value left behind. In revenge, Wu tore down the Sui ancestral gate and erected another of his own, the one you see here."

"But why should he have done that?" asked Chen, looking puzzled.

"Why, to destroy all trace of the Sui clan, and to bring upon himself the *Feng Shui* that had caused his rival to prosper. But the Wu family never prospered. Treachery and childlessness seem to have brought the line almost to an end: and, it seems, the Lady Wu will be the last to bear the clan name."

Liu Hua shuddered. "It seems that I have inherited a curse, as well as a ruined mansion and a worthless title."

The notary shrugged his shoulders. "You're going to do some rebuilding, obviously. So why not ask the *Feng Shui* expert's advice? It might all work out for the best."

Chen looked over the rotted wood, the crumbling plaster, and the broken masonry, and put on a brave smile. "It needs only time and money."

"And we haven't much of either," said his wife, shaking her head.

Chen hugged his wife, and pointed to their children, who by now had found a way into the overgrown courtyard. "Look, Liu Hua. See how happy they are! Isn't it worth it for them? They think it's the next step to Heaven, being here."

Liu Hua, however, could not settle easily. It seemed to her that in some way she had betrayed her husband, although he was cheerful enough.

It was only when Chen mentioned that he would have to employ outside help to restore the main gate that the idea suddenly occurred to her. "Chen, do you remember the old legend that the notary told us? Couldn't we put the main gate exactly where it was in the olden days?"

Chen looked at her in surprise. "But that would be almost impossible. Apart from the cost of rebuilding, all the extra work and all the time involved, we don't even know where the gate would have stood."

Liu Hua pondered deeply. "I'm sure someone would be able to find out where the site of the old gateway was. The geomancer, he would be the one to know."

*   *   *

The *Feng Shui* master scratched his beard. "Do I understand you clearly? You are rebuilding your house, but you wish to erect your gateway according to the horoscope of someone else? Your revered ancestor, perhaps? No? Your wife's then?"

"Neither mine, nor my wife's, nor indeed anyone known to me: but the Lord of Sui, if such a person ever actually existed."

The *Feng Shui* master drew his breath, sharply. "In Heaven, all things are known; but for Man, the wonders are unending."

It was many minutes before he spoke again. "There are historians in the town who possess ancient annals. These may give details of the original mansion, but I doubt it. They usually list only the names of notable personalities, and their important deeds. But if they give the Lord of Sui's date of birth, I will be able to calculate his horoscope. Then I can advise you on the direction which the new gate must face. But suppose it creates a bad *Feng Shui* for yourself, what then?"

"That does not matter," replied Chen. "My wife, now the Lady Wu, believes that her family owes a debt to the Sui ancestor, and wishes to repay it. The mansion is not mine, neither by purchase nor inheritance. If, in restoring the *Feng Shui* for the Lord of Sui, it should prove to be adverse for me, then so be it."

"Your wishes are truly virtuous," said the *Feng Shui* master, solemnly. "Let us hope that the *Feng Shui* of the Lord of Sui will bring honour to you also. You are from Shanghai, I believe?"

"I lived there, yes, but was born in Wuhan."

For a moment, the *Feng Shui* master appeared startled, but then calmly asked for Chen's date of birth.

"I will need a few days to research the annals of the families of Wu and Sui. Then perhaps we will be able to judge the best location for the main gate, and the orientation of the rooms. It will also be important to decide on the most auspicious day to erect the first timbers for the new gate. All this may not be for a month or more. Meanwhile, may your efforts be fruitful."

*   *   *

As it turned out, the *Feng Shui* master was indeed able to find the date of birth of the Lord of Sui in the ancient annals. He also drew up plans for the new gateway, and sketched the mansion, showing the best situation for each room. Work progressed steadily, until Chen made an astonishing discovery. He immediately sent for the *Feng Shui* master, but to his surprise found that the scholar had already arrived.

"My respects to your ancestors, Sir. I trust that all is ready for tomorrow? The next auspicious day for the erection of the timbers will not be for three months."

"Whatever your advice, you can be sure I will heed it." Chen replied. "We have made an amazing discovery. Thanks to your careful calculations, we have unearthed the actual foundations of the original gateway. And even at this moment, the ground is being cleared so that a new gateway can be erected at the exact spot where it stood all those centuries ago."

The *Feng Shui* master lowered his head in modest acknowledgement. "It was due more to Heaven's ordinance than any skill of mine, Sir." He was about to continue further, when at that moment there was a shout from the workmen who were digging the foundations.

Chen ran to the trench, peered in, and stared in astonishment. Liu Hua, attracted by the noise, hurried over, too. Alarmed by the look on her husband's face, she leaned over to see what lay there. The *Feng Shui* master was the last to arrive. He addressed Chen respectfully.

"Until this moment, I could only surmise. But now I am certain. This is surely the ordinance of Heaven. My researches reveal that when the Lord of Sui was unlawfully expelled, he spent his exile in Wuhan, where your Honour was born. But he did not take his treasure with him. Instead he buried it beneath the ancestral gateway, here, in the place where only his rightful descendant would find it."

The Compass school of *Feng Shui* has an even wider application than the correct siting of buildings and the planning of their interiors, since for many Far Eastern peoples, not only the Chinese, a vital aspect of *Feng Shui* also concerns the question of the correct direction to take when embarking on a journey, as well as the determining of favourable days. Before setting off for a crucial business meeting, an almanac will often be consulted, both to ascertain the most beneficial route to take, and also to select the most propitious time for discussing a deal with a client. Indeed, it has been known for canny European traders, resident in the Far East, to consult the relevant sections of the Chinese Almanac before arranging any appointments, not because they gave any credence to its judgements, but because they knew it would be impractical to arrange a meeting at a time which the Chinese considered to be inauspicious.

Everyone, whether stationary or in motion, is at the crossroads of the two sciences, astrology and *Feng Shui*. The former is the study of celestial influences revealed by the positions of the stars and other heavenly bodies, and consequently the counterpoint to *Feng Shui*, which is the study of both the beneficial and inauspicious influences of the Earth. When you are stationary, the *Feng Shui* influences remain constant, while astrological influences fluctuate according to the constantly changing positions of celestial bodies; but when you are travelling, the *Feng Shui* pattern will also change. And in order to ensure that Heaven and Earth are in harmony, *time* and *direction* must be in accord.

Time is measured by the calendar, *direction* by the compass, and the concordance between *time* and *direction* by the Chinese *Feng Shui* instrument, known as the *Lo P'an* or 'grid plate'.

For the geomancer, the *Lo P'an* is as indispensable as a stethoscope to a doctor. This instrument (sometimes also called the *Lo Ching*) has two parts: a circular 'Heaven Plate' (the 'working' part of the *Lo P'an*), and a base or 'Earth Plate', into which the Heaven Plate fits. Although the base plate is quite plain, distinguished only by its two cross threads, the Heaven Plate needs to have some form of base plate as a point of reference before the *Lo P'an* can be employed. For this purpose, there are two red threads which run from the middle of each side of the Earth Plate, crossing at right angles directly over the central point of the Heaven Plate.

In the Chinese *Lo P'an*, the circular 'Heaven Plate' has a magnetic compass needle in the centre, surrounded by several concentric rings, marked into divisions, most of which are inscribed with Chinese characters. The number of rings varies considerably. The smallest *Lo P'an* may have three or four; the largest, several dozen. In addition to their *Feng Shui* role, some rings provide the combined functions of a geographical compass and a surveyor's protractor. The more complex *Lo P'an* also incorporates a basic astronomical planisphere, indicating the principal constellations and Chinese degree divisions, which represent every day of the year. The *Feng Shui* expert sometimes uses these divisions to decide the most propitious date for commencement of work on a site or the opening of a building, while astronomers can also use the instrument to determine the position of the stars for any given moment.

Early forms of *Lo P'an* were made from baked clay, pear-wood, or lacquer. Today, those manufactured in China and exported throughout the Far East, both for the tourist trade and the professional *Feng Shui* practitioner, are made mainly from light-coloured wood, set in a varnished 'Earth Plate'. A source in Fo Shan in South China produces inexpensive versions, also made of varnished wood, but covered with printed paper. Throughout the Far East, however, there can be found very superior models, cast in enamelled brass, and varying in size from a few centimetres in diameter to the largest surveyor's *Lo P'an*, nearly a metre across. These very expensive instruments (in 1987, the largest example cost the equivalent of nearly two thousand US dollars) are manufactured in Kaohsiung, in the Republic of China (Taiwan).

The *Lo P'an* has always had the great disadvantage to the Western user of being inscribed entirely in Chinese characters. Now, however, that difficulty has been solved by the Western adaptation of the *Lo P'an* given on page 85. It needs only to be supplemented by an ordinary Western compass; and even that may be dispensed with if the direction of North is known for the locality.

Magic Measurements

Many *Feng Shui* specialists believe that certain dimensions and proportions encourage good fortune. For this reason, Chinese carpenters, masons, and geomancers often employ a distinctive *Ting Lan* ruler showing which measurements are auspicious, and which ones should be avoided. Its unit of measurement, however, is unique. It is, in fact, the length of the diagonal of a square, the side of which is one Chinese foot (almost identical to the standard imperial foot). This factor, the square root of two, known to Western mathematicians as the 'Golden Section', was considered by the Chinese to have mystical significance.

But unlike the standard Chinese foot, which is divided into ten Chinese inches, the *Feng Shui* foot of the *Ting Lan* ruler is divided into eight, in order that each division may correspond with one of the Eight Trigrams. However, only one of the sections, the third, *Li*, ('Separation') still keeps its original trigram name, the others now being known instead by their particular portents.

The *Feng Shui* foot is virtually 43cms (about 17ins); and it is no coincidence that the standard size brief-case made in the Far East should be exactly this length, since this is meant to ensure that the paper and documents it holds are surrounded by prosperity. For measurements greater than one *Feng Shui* foot, portents are taken from the remaining eighths: thus for a measurement of, say, 4⅝ *Feng Shui* feet, the portents would be those of the fifth division

('Promotion'), indicating that a door or window of this size would stimulate success in career. The joiner or builder will use standard measurements, but plan the work in hand so that all dimensions fall well within the boundaries of the favourable sections of the geomantic ruler which has auspicious measurements given in red; the less propitious ones, in black.

The Eight Divisions of the *Feng Shui* foot and their portents			
Division	**Measurement**	**Name**	**Portent**
I	0 – 5.4 cms (2⅛ ins)	*Ts'ai*	Wealth
II	5.5 – 10.7 cms (4¼ ins)	*Ping*	Sickness
III	10.8 – 16.1 cms (6⁵⁄₁₆ ins)	*Li*	Separation
IV	16.2 – 21.4 cms (8⁷⁄₁₆ ins)	*I*	Righteousness
V	21.5 – 26.8 cms (10½ ins)	*Kuan*	Promotion
VI	26.9 – 32.1 cms (12⅝ ins)	*Chieh*	Robbery
VII	32.2 – 37.5 cms (14¾ ins)	*Hai*	Accident
VIII	37.5 – 42.9 cms (16¹⁵⁄₁₆ ins)	*Pen*	Source

There is, too, another system of *Feng Shui* measurement, using a different standard of length, and with divisions into ten. *Feng Shui* rulers and measuring tapes usually show these alternative divisions, although they are not in such general use.

The Western Lo P'an

The Western *Lo P'an* includes all the features to be found on the basic Chinese *Lo P'an*, together with some additional refinements which are only found in larger models. Most average-sized Chinese instruments repeat the basic rings, first deflected 7½ degrees to the left, and again 7½ degrees to the right; but by omitting these repetitions, it has been possible to allocate space to other interesting features. A description of each ring of the Western *Lo P'an* is given below. The letters in square brackets refer to the markings on the cursor template, provided on page 86, and for use with the *Lo P'an*.

Centre [A] and [B]
The Heaven Pool

At the centre of a Chinese *Lo P'an* is a magnetic compass, known as the 'Heaven Pool', with the needle pointing Southwards, in traditional fashion. The Heaven Pool is inscribed with a reference line on its base, shown here in the Western *Lo P'an* as a double pointer.

When using the Western *Lo P'an*, it is essential that point [A] on the cursor touches the central pivot [A] of the Heaven Pool [B].

Ring [C]
The Eight Trigrams

The Eight Trigrams, bordering the Heaven Pool, appear here in the 'Former Heaven' sequence, the order normally found on the Chinese *Lo P'an*, but not in the order found on a Chinese mariner's compass. Their purpose on the *Lo P'an* is almost exclusively talismanic. The Heaven Pool pointer links trigrams *Ch'ien* [☰] and *K'un* [☷].

Ring [D]
The Twelve Animals

The twelve double-hours of the Chinese day are sometimes known by the names of the twelve animals of the Chinese zodiac: Rat, Ox, Tiger, Hare, Dragon, Snake, Horse, Sheep, Monkey, Rooster, Dog and Pig.

Their function here is the same as that of the Twelve Branches in the next ring [E], and their inclusion is a useful mnemonic.

Ring [E]
The Twelve Branches of the Double-Hours

The twelve animals are a popular way of representing the Twelve Branches, used to calculate the twelve Double-Hours of the day, and identified here by the Roman numerals I-XII. Branch I represents the midnight double-hour; Branch VII, noon. Note that midnight and noon are the mid-points of their respective double-hours. Thus, double-hour I is from 11pm to 1am.

Ring [F]
The Compass Points

The Chinese divide the compass face into twenty-four parts, which do not all correspond with the subdivisions of the Western compass. As with the Double-Hours, the critical point of each division is its centre. They are represented in this Western *Lo P'an* by a sequence of Roman numerals I-XII, ordinary figures 1-10 (omitting 5 and 6 since these are associated with the Earth and centre) and four of the Eight Trigrams.

Ring [G]
The Twenty-four Solar Fortnights

In the Chinese calendar, the true solar year is divided into twenty-four equal parts, each about fifteen days long, beginning with 4th February but actually calculated from the Winter Solstice, on 21/22 December.

Ring [H]
The Five Elements

There are sixty divisions in this ring, each marked with a symbol for one of the Five Elements: ▮ Wood; ▲ Fire; ■ Earth; ◣ Metal; ⚬⚬ Water. Traditionally, there are sixty-one irregular divisions. For the Western *Lo P'an*, the divisions have been regularly spaced, retaining the original positions of each of the Five Elements as closely as possible.

Ring [I]
The Sixty Dragons

The figures 1 to 10 represent the Ten Daily Stems of the Chinese calendar, repeated in different sequences.

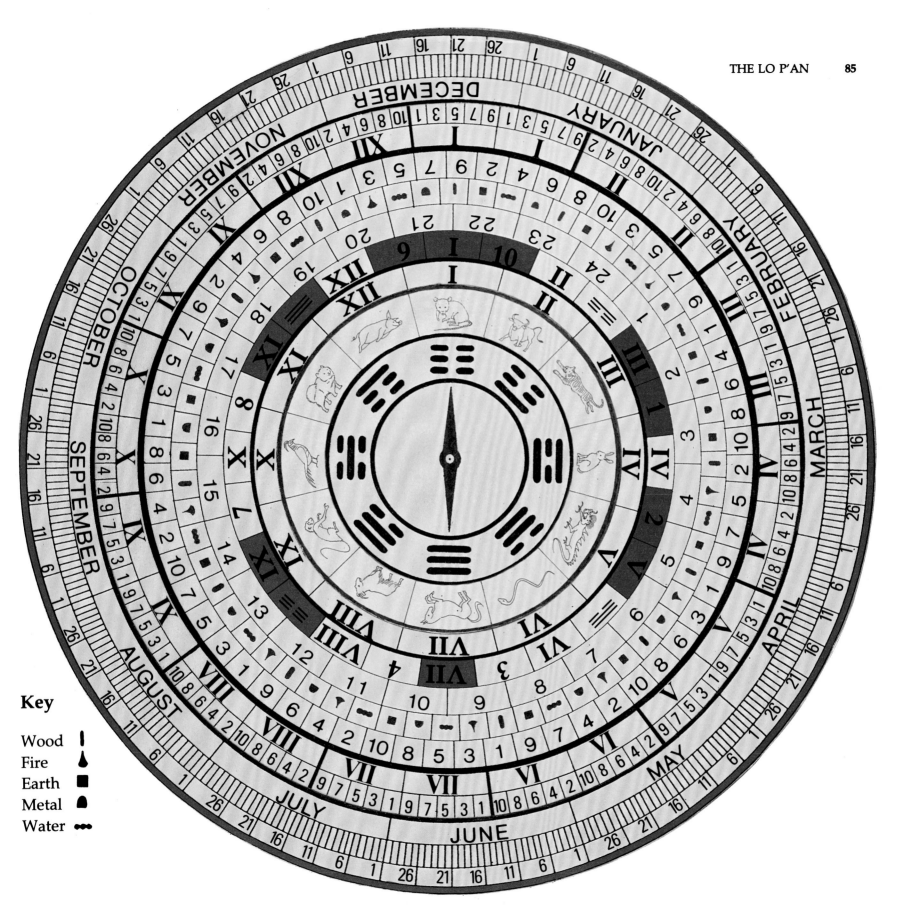

Key

Wood ┃

Fire ◭

Earth ■

Metal ◖

Water •••

Their function in this ring is for the calculation of the critical orientation of a building in order to maximize the beneficial influences of the Dragon in the surrounding landscape.

Ring [J]
The Twelve Branches of the Days
These divisions, marked in Roman numerals, combine with the Ten Daily Stems to number the days of the Chinese calendar, and are used to calculate fortunate days and directions.

Ring [K]
The 120 Dragons or Feng Chin
A further arrangement of the Ten Daily Stems is used in calculating the relative favourability of the landscape.

Right [L]
The Western Months
Divisions of the year are given in this Western adaptation of the *Lo P'an* according to Western months, and are further divided into day divisions in ring [M].

Ring [M]
Division into Chinese Degrees
The Chinese divide the circle into 365¼ degrees, so that each degree corresponds to one day's movement of the progression of the sun through the sky. As this virtually corresponds to the Western calendar, this final ring conveniently functions as a Chinese protractor and a Western calendar disc, and can be used for finding the directions which harmonize with any particular day, as well as for calculating *Feng Shui* horoscopes.

Using the Western Lo P'an

In the Chinese *Lo P'an*, the Heaven Plate is set in the Earth Plate and rotated until the North-South pointer line of the Heaven Plate matches one of the guide or cursor threads of the Earth Plate. In this Western version of the *Lo P'an*, turning the book has the same result as rotating the Heaven Plate, and a cursor, described below, functions as the Earth Plate.

You will first need to make the cursor. Take a strip of paper with a straight clean-cut edge, and lay the edge against the cursor template given here.

Mark the edge of the paper with points and letters to match those on the cursor template.

You will need to know the direction of North. This can be ascertained with an ordinary compass, or from personal knowledge of the locality.

Basic procedure

1 Place this open book on a convenient flat surface. Turn the book until the central pointer of the Heaven Pool is aligned North-South, the Rat in the North position. Ensure that the open book is kept securely in position. The Rat should *always* be at North.

2 Take the cursor, and place its edge on the Heaven Plate with the mark [A] at the central pivot. The letters marked on the cursor will then identify each of the rings on the Heaven Plate. Always ensure that the point [A] of the cursor is at the central pivot of the *Lo P'an*.

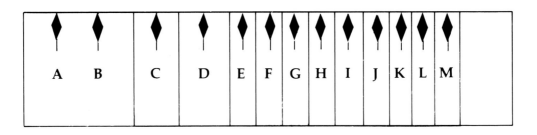

Initial calculations

In order to use the *Lo P'an* as described in the Examples on pages 92-97, it will be necessary to work through a number of initial steps, outlined as follows:

To determine the Solar Fortnight for any date

The Solar Fortnight is a factor in the calculation of the Natal Number. The Natal Number is a figure which will be found to have great importance when calculating individual *Feng Shui* horoscopes – as, for instance, in Example 3 on page 93 . Place the cursor over the given date at ring [M] and note the figure shown in ring [G]. Now refer to Table 4 on page 104 .

To determine the Natal Trigram

The method for calculating the trigrams for the rooms of a building and the trigram for the date of birth is as follows.

Note: As the Chinese Day is reckoned from 11pm, not midnight, any time between 11pm and midnight should be counted as the next day.

Take a sheet of paper, and down the left-hand side, in a column, write the letters **A** to **I**.

A Note the year of birth, and then turn to the Table of Dates of the Chinese New Year on page 102. (If the birth date occurs before the Chinese New Year, subtract 1 from the birth-year date.) Write the year of birth, adjusted if necessary, at **A** on your worksheet. (*Example:* Date of birth, 30th January 1956. As 30th January occurs before the Chinese New Year in 1956, take the previous year as the birth year. The adjusted year is thus 1955.)

B To calculate the Annual Number:
For a man:
Take the last two figures of the number at **A**.
Divide by 9.
Subtract the remainder from 10. (If the answer is 0, call this 1.)
For a woman:
Take the last two figures of the number at **A**. Add 5.
Divide by 9, and note the remainder. (If the remainder is 0, call this 9.)
The final answer is the Annual Number. Enter the Annual Number at **B**.

C Using the *Lo P'an* (there is no need to adjust the book to the North-South direction), place the cursor over the date of birth in the outer ring [M], and read off the Fortnight Number from ring [G]. Enter this figure at **C**.

D Turn to Table 4 on page 104 (The Twenty-Four Solar Fortnights). Find the Fortnight Number (**C** on your work-sheet) in the left-hand column of the table. Then find which column on the right is headed with the relevant Annual Number (**B** on your work-sheet.) Cross-refer to find the Natal Number. Enter this on your work-sheet at **D**.

E From Table 3 on page 103, find the trigram corresponding to the Natal Number (**D** on your work-sheet). Note this at **E**.

F From Table 3 on page 103, it will also be seen that each trigram has a Type (Easterly or Westerly), Direction, Polarity, and Element. Note these at **F,G,H**, and **I** on your work-sheet.

It is generally favourable for Easterly-type people to be positioned in *Yang* directions, and Westerly types to be positioned in *Yin* directions. This rule can be observed in the allocation of bedrooms within a household, or the disposition of guests at the dining-table.

Similarly, when moving house, or re-locating for business or other purposes, it is more favourable to move towards those directions, *Yang* or *Yin*, which are appropriate to Easterly or Westerly types, respectively.

To compare the trigrams of the house with the trigram of the individual

In order to find out whether a particular part of the building or a room of a house is auspicious for a particular person, the Element of the trigram of the room must be compared with the Element of the trigram of the individual.

Refer once again to the Table of Natal Numbers on page 103, and the sequence of the Elements on page 89. If the Element of the trigram of the room *produces* the Element pertaining to the trigram of the individual, this is auspicious; but if the Element of the trigram of the room immediately precedes the Element of the trigram of the individual in the *destructive* sequence, then this is considered to be unfavourable. If the Elements match, this is also favourable. Otherwise the portents are neither particularly favourable nor disadvantageous.

You may, for instance, wish to know if a West-facing room is auspicious for you. To do this, you will need to compare the trigram of the room with your own trigram. Your Natal Number, suppose, is 1. This pertains to the Element Water. (See Table 3 on page 103). The West-facing room pertains to the Element Metal. (See Table 3 on page 103). As Metal generates Water, the room is therefore auspicious. This would not be the case however, for someone whose Natal Number is 4, since the number 4 pertains to the Element Earth, said to destroy Water.

To find the Stem-and-Branch for any Western date

Take a piece of paper, and write the letters **J-M** in a column down the left-hand side.

J   From Table 2 on page 103, note the code number for the Year at **J**.

K   Turn to Table 7 on page 107, and find the required month and date. Note the figure in the left-hand column and enter this at **K**.

L   Add the figure at **K** to the code number for the year at **J**. (If the required date occurs on or after 29th February in a leap year, add 1). If the total is greater than 61, subtract 60. Write the result at **L**.

M   The figure at **L** is the number of the Stem-and-Branch combinations in the complete series listed in Table 6 on page 106. Write the Stem-and-Branch at **M**.

To find the Western dates for a given Stem-and-Branch

Again, take a piece of paper, and write the letters **N-Q** in a column down the left-hand side.

N   Find the Stem-and-Branch combination in the list given on page 106, and note the figure at **N**.

O   Turn to Table 1 on page 102, and note the code number for the year at **O**. If this figure is greater than the Stem-and-Branch number at **N**, add 60 to the Stem-and-Branch number at **N**. Write this figure at **O**.

P   Subtract the year code number at **O** from the figure at **N** to give the code number for the required date, and write this at **P**.

Q   Turn to Table 7 on page 107. Find the code number at **P** in the left-hand column, and note the choice of dates which are alongside. The required Stem-and-Branch will fall on each of those dates. *Note: In leap years, for dates after February 28, read next date.*

List of portents

The direction which the entrance faces is regarded as the orientation of the building as a whole. Each of the remaining seven directions possesses a different portent, according to the direction of the entrance. The seven portents are:

1 **Seven Imps** *Inauspicious* Troublesome, disease, headaches, petty annoyances.

2 **Six Ghosts** *Inauspicious* Such rooms may have a 'creepy' feeling to them.

3 **Conclusion** *Inauspicious* Not suitable for sick people.

4 **Longevity** *Very auspicious* Ideal for health.

5 **Disaster** *Inauspicious* Accidents, or loss of office, may accrue from spending long periods in this room.

6 **Vitality** *Very auspicious* Ideal for energising.

7 **Celestial Physician** *Very auspicious* Ideal situation for placing invalids to speed their recovery.

How these seven portents are allocated to the Eight Directions can be seen in the charts on page 105.

Interpreting the Elements

When a feature of the landscape has a shape which can be readily identified as one of the Elemental shapes described on page 32, the *Lo P'an* can be used to evaluate its influence at a particular site or within a building.

Set up the *Lo P'an* at the required location. Examine the skyline for features such as knolls, summits of hills, water-towers, pylons, high buildings, and other prominences. Point the cursor towards the skyline feature, and then note the Element of the location which is on the *opposite* side of the *Lo P'an* at ring [H].

Note whether the Element of the skyline feature is harmonious with the Element of the location, shown by the *Lo P'an*, or whether it is injurious, in which case a *controlling* Element should be introduced.

A feature can be considered harmonious if the Element of the feature *immediately* precedes the Element of the location in the following *productive* sequence:

Productive Sequence

Wood→Fire→Earth→Metal→Water→Wood

But a feature is injurious if the Element of the feature *immediately* precedes the Element of the location in the following *destructive* sequence:

Destructive Sequence

Wood→Earth→Water→Fire→Metal→Wood

If the Elements of the feature and the location do not stand in any of the above two relationships, the *Feng Shui* influence is neither beneficial nor unfavourable.

Controlling unfavourable Element features

When the Element of the feature is one which will destroy the Element of the location, its bad influence can be averted by positioning something representing the *controlling* Element in the required position. The *controlling* Element is the one which preceeds the *threatened* Element in the *productive* sequence above. Thus, if the Element of the feature is Metal, and the Element of the location, shown by the *Lo P'an*, is Wood, then it is said that physical or financial weakness will result as surely as Metal chops down Wood. At the spot under the influence of the adverse feature, it will therefore be necessary to have something representing the *controlling* Element – in this case, Water. (Water is seen to precede Wood in the *productive* sequence.)

The five combinations of adverse situations can be summarised as follows:

Metal feature/Wood location This is said to result in physical and financial weakness. The *controlling* Element is Water; so an aquarium, vase of flowers, or water-dispenser might be placed at the spot.

Earth feature/Water location This is said to bring illness and disease. The *controlling* Element is Metal, so something Metal should be introduced.

Water feature/Fire location This is said to indicate illness in young children. The *controlling* Element is Wood. Books or papers may be placed in position to control the weakening influence of Water.

Fire feature/Metal location This is regarded as a portent of accidents. The *controlling* Element, Earth, may be represented by bonsai or cactus gardens, or clay, pottery or porcelain figures.

Wood feature/Earth location This is said to presage loss of office, or unemployment. To avert such calamity, as the *controlling* Element is Fire, a fireplace or something representing the Element Fire, in a bright red colour, should be placed at the location.

To interpret the Dragon

When planning a site or investigating the *Feng Shui* of an existing building, the geomancer will examine the surrounding landscape for promising Dragon features. Once a suitable Dragon has been identified, its maximum benefit can be derived by knowing the critical direction through which its influences are felt.

First, identify the Dragon. Then place the cursor on the *Lo P'an* so that it is in line with the Dragon feature. Note the Stem indicated at ring [I], and examine the Table of Dragon Stems, right. If the alignment indicates an unfavourable Stem, adjust the cursor to cross ring [I] at the nearest favourable Stem in either direction.

When a favourable Stem has been established, note the figure/symbol at ring [F] which refers to a Chinese compass direction. (*See* page 91.) If the direction at ring [F] is red, it is the direction which receives the greatest benefits. If the direction is not red, there is neither benefit nor harm. Further adjustment can then be made to arrive at a direction which harmonises with both the Stem and compass direction.

Table of Dragon Stems	
Stem	*Quality*
1	*Unlucky too oppressive and dominating*
2	*Unlucky too demanding*
3	*Lucky positive, prosperous*
4	*Lucky accepting and helping*
5	*Stable position, no influences felt*
6	*Stable position, no influences felt*
7	*Lucky actively prosperous*
8	*Lucky encouraging*
9	*Unlucky dominating*
10	*Unlucky weakening*

In the case of Stems 5 and 6, the favourable influences of the Dragon do not have any effect, but *Feng Shui* consultants would usually regard them as being unfavourable, rather than neutral. When a Dragon may not be readily apparent, align the cursor in turn with various prominences on the skyline, noting the number of the Dragon Stem at ring [I] and again comparing this with the Table of Dragon Stems, shown here. An example of how this procedure can be put into practice is given on page 97.

The Chinese Compass

The Chinese compass – ring [F] on the Western version of the *Lo P'an* on page 85 – is divided into twenty-four sections. As the Western compass divides successively by two into sixteen or thirty-two, this means that it is not possible to make an exact match between the two systems. Furthermore, in the Chinese system, each division occupies fifteen degrees of angular measurement – so that, for example, by 'North' the Chinese indicate the sector between 7½° East and 7½° West of North.

The twenty-four divisions combine four of the Eight Trigrams, eight of the Ten Heavenly Stems, and each of the Twelve Earthly Branches. On larger examples of the Chinese *Lo P'an*, these will all appear in separate rings of the Heaven Plate: but in smaller versions, and in the Western adaptation on page 85, they are combined together in one ring [F].

The twenty-four compass points are all shown in position in the first outer ring of the diagram right. The Twelve Earthly Branches are distributed round the face of the compass regularly, as shown in the second ring from the outside, with I, IV, VII, and X at the N, E, S, and W points respectively, and the other Branches interposed.

The four trigrams – *Ken*, *Sun*, *K'un* and *Ch'ien* – appear at the four 'corners', mid-way between the cardinal points at NE, SE, SW, and NW respectively, as shown in the central ring. (The term 'corner' is actually a direct translation of the Chinese term.)

The remaining eight places are taken by eight of the Ten Heavenly Stems, as seen in the third

ring from the outside. Stems 5 and 6, associated with the Element Earth, and so not regarded as appropriate for the Heaven Plate, are omitted. Coincidentally, the Chinese characters for Stems 5 and 6 are very easily confused with the characters for Branches XI and VI, so their omission is therefore very practical, too. The eight Stems proceed in a clockwise order, Stem 1 appearing in the place after Branch III.

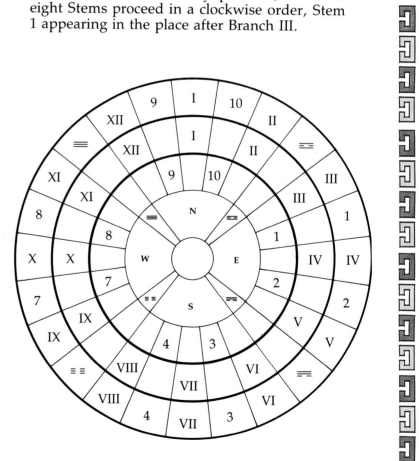

To match your home to your horoscope

The basic principles of *Feng Shui* have been refined over the ages, so that the lay-out of houses and commercial buildings may be tailor-made to match the horoscope of the principal resident or proprietor. Horoscopes are considered to favour particular and perhaps differing directions. So it follows that the location of rooms within a building, according to their orientation and situation, may be more or less favourable for different members of the household.

Each of the Eight Trigrams represents one of the eight major compass directions. (These are listed on page 41). One of the trigrams may thus be allotted to each room of a building according to its location relative to the entrance. For example, a room situated to the East of the main entrance is regarded as *Chen*, this being the trigram associated with the East.

Additionally, everyone's horoscope (represented by the date of birth) can also be reduced to a trigram. If this trigram matches or harmonizes with the trigram of the room, then that room will be favourable for the individual.

The following examples feature step-by-step instructions for most of the *Feng Shui* calculations you are likely to require. They can be readily used as models for similar situations.

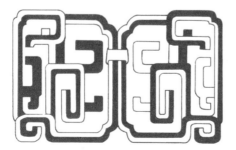

Practical Examples

1 To determine the most suitable orientation for a building, when the date of birth of the principal occupier is known

John Grigson was born on 8th October 1939. He is having a new house built. Which would be the most suitable direction for it to face?

From the Table for the Dates of the Chinese New Year on page 102, it can be seen that the Chinese year in which 8th October 1939 occurs is the Year of the Earth-Hare. Turn to the Western version of the *Lo P'an* on page 85. Following the instructions on page 86, with the Rat at North, place the cursor so that the point D is over the sector featuring the Hare. Now move the cursor through the width of this sector; and from ring [F], note the three Chinese compass directions (numbers) which are found in the Hare sector. These are Chinese compass directions 1, IV (due East) and 2. The directions occupied by Stems 1 and 2, being shown in red, are more favourable than the direction shown by Branch IV.

The entrance to John Grigson's house should ideally be placed in accordance with the directions shown by the cursor when over the segments 1 and 2 in ring [F].

2 To find the *controlling* Element in order to remedy an adverse *Feng Shui* situation

Jane French works in a small office with two other people. Although her desk is placed sideways to the window, it occupies a central position in the room. Through the window, due East, the view is dominated by a large telegraph pole, transmitting – according to Feng Shui principles – ominous 'sha'. Unfortunately, she is not able to alter the position of her desk. What should she do to improve the Feng Shui?

In this instance, in addition to the cursor, a ruler or other long, straight edge, which can cover the whole width of the *Lo P'an*, is needed.

First, the position of North must be ascertained. Next, the *Lo P'an* should be placed on the desk as close as possible to the actual spot where work is done, and the book turned until aligned with the Rat to the North.

The cursor is then laid over the *Lo P'an* so that it points to the offending distant object – in this case, the telegraph pole, due East, within Chinese compass bearing IV on ring [F]. The extra straight edge is positioned along the line of the cursor, and the cursor turned through 180° so that it meets the other end of the straight edge on the side of the *Lo P'an* furthest from the exterior feature. Note the Element symbol at ring *[H]*. This is Earth.

The telegraph pole is represented by the Element Wood. As can be seen from the *destructive* sequence of Elements on page 89, Earth is destroyed by Wood. From the *productive* sequence of Elements, it can be seen that Earth is produced by Fire. Thus, the *controlling* Element in this instance is Fire.

Jane French might therefore offset the baleful *Feng Shui* effect, produced by the telegraph pole, by placing a bright red ornament or utility on her desk to represent the Element Fire.

---

3 To allocate the rooms of a house, thereby matching the home to the horoscope

---

Margaret Kent, born on 4th January 1962, has just bought an apartment in New Jersey. It faces South-West. There are two principal rooms: one faces East, and the other, West. According to Feng Shui principles, it is essential for the bedroom to be auspiciously situated. Which room, therefore, would be the most favourable?

Margaret's apartment faces South-West: and from the chart showing the Eight Orientations of Buildings on page 105, we see that, in a South-West type of building, the portent number for West (the direction faced by one room) is 7, and for East (the direction faced by the other), 5. Turning to the list of portents on page 89, we see that 7 is referred to as *'Celestial Physician*, very auspicious, and an ideal situation for placing invalids to speed their recovery.' The portent for 5 is referred to as *'Disaster*, inauspicious, and indicating accidents, or loss of office accruing from spending long periods in this room'. The Western room is therefore the more auspicious of the two.

It is now necessary to consider Margaret's horoscope. Examine the Table of the Dates of the Chinese New Year on page 102 to see whether Margaret was born before the Chinese New Year in 1962. In that year, the Chinese year began on 5th February. 1961 is therefore taken as the birth year.

The next stage of the calculation involves determining the Natal Number for the individual, as detailed on page 87.

Since the occupant is female, add 5 to the last two figures of the birth year (61). This gives 66 which, divided by 9, gives a remainder of 3. The Annual Number is therefore 3.

It is then necessary to find the Solar Fortnight Number. Using the *Lo P'an* (there is no need to orientate it), place the cursor to align with 4th January. The figure at ring *[G]* is seen to be 22.

Turn to the Table of The Twenty-Four Solar Fortnights on page 104. Alongside the Fortnight Number 22, in the column headed Female/Annual Number 3, is the figure 2. This is therefore Margaret Kent's Natal Number.

From the Table of Natal Numbers on page 103, we find that, for 2, the trigram is *K'un*; type, Westerly; direction, South-West; polarity, *Yin*; and the Element, Earth.

From the Table of Natal Numbers on page 103, we see that the Element of West is Metal. From the Table showing the *destructive* order of the Elements on page 89, it is clear that Metal is not harmful to Earth (the Element of Margaret's Natal Number). Similarly, from the Table of Natal Numbers, it can be ascertained that the Element of the East is Wood. Wood destroys Earth, as you will again see from page 89. This is, therefore, an additional reason for avoiding the Easterly-situated room for the bedroom.

4 To allocate the rooms of a new office building

John Sharif, born 23rd September 1950, is the managing director of an advertising agency which has taken over the complete floor of a skyscraper building on the North side of a major road. How should he plan the area so that his own office suite derives the maximum Feng Shui potential?

As the building is on the North side of the avenue, it faces South. There are two things to consider: the general lay-out of the suite, and its interaction with the managing director's horoscope.

Identify the diagram of the South-facing building among the charts showing the Eight Orientations of Buildings on page 105. Here, you will find the portent numbers for each direction. Referring to the list of portents on page 89, the portents for each direction are found to be as follows:

North	4	Longevity	*Very auspicious*
North-East	5	Disaster	*Inauspicious*
East	6	Vitality	*Very auspicious*
South-East	7	Celestial Physician	*Very auspicious*
South		(Entrance)	
South-West	1	Seven Imps	*Inauspicious*
West	2	Six Ghosts	*Inauspicious*
North-West	3	Conclusion	*Inauspicious*

Proceed according to the method for finding the Natal Number on page 87. The last two figures of John Sharif's birth-year (which does not need to be adjusted as his date-of-birth occurs after the Chinese New Year in 1950) are found to be 50. As we are doing a calculation for a man, divide this by 9. This leaves a remainder of 5. Subtract 5 from 10, to give 5, John's Annual Number.

From the *Lo P'an* ring [G], the Solar Fortnight Number for 23rd September is seen to be 16. From the Table of the Twenty-Four Solar Fortnights on page 104 in the column headed Male Annual Number 5, alongside 16 is the Natal Number 4. From the Table of Natal Numbers and their Attributes on page 103, John's trigram is seen to be *Sun*; and his Element, Wood. From the *productive* order of the Elements on page 89, we know that the Element producing Wood is Water.

From the Table of Natal Numbers and their Attributes on page 103, it can be seen that Water (the Element which produces John's Element, Wood) is associated with the direction North.

North will therefore be the most appropriate side of the building for John's own suite, including his secretary's office, as this direction *produces* his Natal Element. From the list of portents opposite, it is also clear that North is very auspicious in a South-oriented building. So rooms might be allocated in the following way:

North	Longevity	*Managing director's suite*
North-East	Disaster	*Cloakrooms*
East	Vitality	*Drawing-office; studios; copywriters; boardroom*
South-East	Celestial Physician	*Account executive; personnel; canteen; first-aid*
South	(Entrance)	
South-West	Seven Imps	*Typing pool; accounts*
West	Six Ghosts	*Store*
North-West	Conclusion	*Despatch*

5 To find favourable days for particular ventures

Michel Lebrun, born on 20th November 1955, is opening a garden centre just outside Paris. It is expected to be ready sometime in 1990. What would be the best day to invite the Press to its opening?

Numerous people are being invited, so a day is required which is favourable generally. However, as the day ought to bring maximum benefit to M. Lebrun, it should be as compatible as possible with his own date of birth.

First, it is necessary to find the Stem-and-Branch pertaining to M. Lebrun's own date of birth.

Following the instructions on page 88 for finding the Stem-and-Branch for any Western date, from the table giving code numbers for the years 1901-2000 on page 103, it can be seen that the year code for 1955 is 58. The date of birth is 20th November. From the Table of Stem-and-Branch Codes on page 107, we ascertain that the relevant code for 20th November is 24.

Add the Stem-and-Branch code 24 to the year code 58. This gives 82. As 82 is greater than 61, subtract 60 from 82. This gives a Stem-and-Branch number of 22.

From the Table of Sequences of Stems-and-Branches on page 106, it can be seen that the Stem-and-Branch combination for number 22 is 2-X.

The next step is to find those days in 1990 which have the same Stem-and-Branch as M. Lebrun's birth-date. For this, the instructions on page 88 for finding the Western date for a given Stem-and-Branch should be followed. The Stem-and-Branch number corresponding to 2-X is already known to be 22.

The year code for 1990, as can be seen from Table of Code Numbers for the Years 1901-2000 on page 103, is 2. (Note that 1990 is not a leap year, so no adjustment is necessary.)

Subtract the year code, 2, from the Stem-and-Branch number 22, to give 20. The Stem-and-Branch code for the required dates in 1990 is thus 20.

Turning again to the Table of Stem-and-Branch Codes on page 107, we find that the dates which have the code 20 are: January 20, March 21, May 20, July 19, September 17, November 16. All these dates will be favourable for M. Lebrun, and thus for opening the garden centre.

The cursor is now placed over these dates in ring [M] of the Lo P'an to select the most appropriate of these dates for the opening of a garden centre. When the cursor is placed over March 21, the direction of the cursor is due East. Of the six dates, March 21 is found to be the only one to harmonise with Wood, since the corresponding Element in ring [H] is Wood; and the Element pertaining to agriculture is obviously Wood. This would, therefore, be the most favourable day of all for the opening of the garden centre.

A similar method can also be used to ascertain the most suitable day for moving house.

6 To find auspicious days and directions for a journey

Dieter Bach, born 12th August 1942 and living in Frankfurt, is considering visiting his grandmother in Zurich. Would it be auspicious for him to travel in this direction on 13th July 1988?

The first step is to consider whether the direction of travel – in this instance, due South – is a favourable one for Dieter Bach. This can be done by comparing the Element of the direction with the Element of his horoscope. For this, it is necessary to calculate the Natal Number. Take the year of birth, 1942; and, following the instructions for a man on page 87, divide 42 by 9. The remainder is 6. Take 6 from 10, to give 4. This is the Annual Number.

Using the Lo P'an (there is no need to orientate it for this calculation), place the cursor to align with the date of birth, 12th August. The figure at ring [G] is seen to be 13. This is the Solar Fortnight Number.

Now turn to the Table of the Twenty-Four Solar Fortnights on page 104. Alongside the Solar Fortnight Number 13 in the column headed Male, Annual Number 4 is the figure 2. This is the Natal Number for Dieter Bach.

From the Table of Natal Numbers and their Attributes on page 103, we find that Dieter Bach's trigram is *K'un*; that he is a Westerly type; that his direction is South-West; his polarity, *Yin*; and his Element, Earth.

From the *productive* order of the Elements given on page 89, it can be seen that the Element producing Earth is Fire. The direction of intended travel is due South. From the Table of Natal Numbers and their Attributes on page 103, it can be seen that South is represented by the Element Fire. So for Dieter Bach, since Fire is the Element which produces his Element, Earth, this would be an auspicious direction generally in which to travel. Furthermore, he is a Westerly type; and from the Table of Natal Numbers and their Attributes on page 103, it can be seen that South is one of the four directions in which it is appropriate for Westerly people to travel.

We shall now consider the proposed date of travel. From the Table of Code Numbers for the Years 1901-2000 on page 103, the code number for 1988 is seen to be 51. As

1988 is a leap year, following the instructions for finding the Stem-and-Branch for any Western date on page 88, add 1, to give 52.

From the Table of Stem-and-Branch Codes on page 107, the code number for the Stem-and-Branch for 13th July is seen to be 14. Add 52 to 14 to give 66. As this figure is greater than 61, subtract 60, to give 6. From the Table of Sequences of Stems-and-Branches on page 106, we see that the Stem-and-Branch number corresponding to 6 is 6-VI. This is the Stem-and-Branch number of Dieter Bach's desired date of travel.

In order to compare the Stem-and-Branch of the desired date of travel with the direction of travel, place the cursor on the *Lo P'an* so that it aligns with each of the two segments representing Stem 6 and Branch VI in rings [K] and [J].

Note the Chinese compass directions at ring [F]. Again there are two positions. These are 3 and VI. As these are not shown in red, they are considered neutral directions. The nearest red section in ring [F] is Chinese compass direction VII. Move the cursor so that [F] is over the Chinese compass direction VII, and note the relevant Stems and Branches at rings [K] and [J]. From the *Lo P'an*, it will be seen that any combination of Stems in ring [K] with Branch VII in ring [J] is auspicious since all fall within the red sector VII in ring [F].

It would therefore be best for Dieter Bach to choose any day with Branch VII for his journey. We have already established that the Branch for the proposed date of travel is Branch VI. As a Branch VII day always follows a Branch VI day, it would be more suitable for him to arrange to make his proposed journey on the following day – that is, on 14th July 1988.

In practice, if this day was not convenient, the inauspicious portents of the day requested could be averted by re-routing the journey in order to travel, initially at least, in the direction pertaining to that day. To find the favourable direction for 13th July, place the cursor over that date in ring [M]. It can be seen that the Chinese compass direction at ring [F] corresponding to this is 4, approximating to SSW. As an alternative, Dieter Bach might therefore set off in this direction on 13th July, before re-routing to the ultimate destination, Zurich.

7 To organise the lay-out for a shop

Anne Glover, born on 11th February 1956, is about to open a greengrocer's shop, which will face West. How should the interior be organised?

Since Anne Glover is the sole owner of the shop, it will be possible to calculate a *Feng Shui* horoscope for her in order to ascertain the ideal interior arrangement.

But before this, certain general statements can be made. From the principles outlined on page 66, it can be seen that a greengrocer's is the 'open' type of shop. The most desirable direction, generally speaking, for the entrance would be in the South-West. Anne's shop, however, faces West, so it would be practicable, as well as favourable from a *Feng Shui* point-of-view, to have the shop entrance placed in the South side of the West wall. A display of goods could then occupy the North section of the West frontage, attracting custom. (If the shop had faced North, Anne could have got around the problem either by arranging her interior display so that customers, on entering, proceeded to the South-West corner, the most desirable point of entrance, or by placing mirrors in the South-West corner to reflect the entrance.)

The next calculation involves determining the ideal position for the cash-point.

Anne's Natal Number can be calculated following the method given on page 87, making sure that the procedure applied to a woman is observed.

From the Table of the Dates of the Chinese New Year on page 102, the New Year for 1956 is seen to be on 12th February. Since Anne's date of birth is prior to this, the year of birth should be regarded as 1955.

Continuing to follow the procedure on page 87, take the last two numbers of the year 1955 and add 5, to give 60. Divide by 9. This gives a remainder of 6, which is therefore the Annual Number. Using the *Lo P'an*, adjust the cursor to cover 11th February in ring [M] and note the corresponding Solar Fortnight marked at ring [G], shown as 1. Under the column headed Female, Annual Number 6, alongside figure 1 in the Solar Fortnight column of the Table of The Twenty-Four Solar Fortnights on page 104 is the figure 1. This is Anne's Natal Number.

From the Table of Natal Numbers on page 103, it can be seen that, for this Natal Number 1, the trigram is *K'an*; the type, Easterly; the direction North; the polarity, *Yang*; and the Element, *Water*. It will be remembered that the Element *producing* the Element for the individual is stimulating and beneficial. It will therefore be favourable for Anne to have the cash-point placed in a location corresponding to the Element producing Water. From the *productive* order of the Elements given on page 89, it can be seen that the Element which produces Water is Metal. Metal is associated with the directions North-West and West, as can be seen from the Table of Natal Numbers and their Attributes on Page 103.

Consequently, the ideal location for Anne to place her cash-point would be in a West or North-West position, conveniently situated for the shop entrance.

---

8 To determine the orientation of a new commercial building

A bank wishes to open new premises in a town with a large Chinese community. It has therefore been decided to employ the services of a Feng Shui expert in order to maintain good relations with its prospective customers. The proposed site faces due South, and there is a well-formed hill, identifiable as a Dragon, in the East. How can the beneficial effect of the Dragon be maximized?

The *Feng Shui* expert, having set up the *Lo P'an*, finds that the Dragon hill is roughly North-East at Chinese compass direction III in ring [F] of the *Lo P'an*.

In ring [I], the Dragon stems corresponding to direction III are found to be 9, 1 and 4. In the Table of Dragon Stems on page 90, these are found to have portents as follows: 9, unlucky; 1, unlucky; 4, lucky.

Therefore, the alignment of the proposed new building should be in a direction corresponding with the favourable direction 4.

Completing a Geomantic Chart

Just as there is no better way to understand any subject than to put it into practice, so the most rewarding way to complete this introduction to *Feng Shui* will be to compile a geomantic chart for your own residence, or that of a friend or relative. This kind of chart is usually drawn up by the geomancer when analysing the location's *Feng Shui*, so that its benefits may be harnessed to the full, and suggestions made to adjust any deficiencies which might be discovered.

A blank geomantic chart is provided on pages 110-111. The following step-by-step instructions explain how to complete and use it. (Readers who do not wish to mark their copy of this book may prefer to make photocopies for their own personal use.)

As a working example, the imaginary case of the Mason family home is used as a model to follow, with the Mason's completed chart shown on pages 108-109.

Method

1 Turn to the geomantic chart on pages 110-111 (or to a photocopy if one has been made), and begin by inserting the name of the principal occupant, the date of birth, the names and relationships of other members of the household, and the address of the residence or building for which the chart is being compiled.

John Mason's date of birth is 2nd January, 1944. He is married to Laura. They have two children, Carol and Paul. The home is at 17 Hill Road.

2 Go to the outside of the building, taking an ordinary compass, a note-book and pencil, and the Western *Lo P'an*, shown on page 85.

Observe the position of North from the compass. Align the *Lo P'an* so that the Rat is in the North position. Now note the prominences and features of the surroundings, paying attention, for example, to hills, high peaks, and natural water features such as streams, lakes, reservoirs, or ponds. In an urban setting, note buildings, large constructions such as bridges, poles, bends in roads, pointed roofs, and other aspects of the skyline, as well as open spaces such as parks and gardens. But wherever the site, only note those features which are observable from the site. Such features which are obscured should not be noted, even though they may be marked on maps of the area. Some features noted will be favourable: others, unfavourable.

Mark these details on the 'Environmental Features' section of the geomantic chart, matching them with the divisions of the Chinese compass, shown in ring [F] of the Western *Lo P'an* on page 85, and on the diagram in this section.

John Mason's house is at the Western end of a terrace. To the North of the house is a small garden and a hill, with a clump of trees at the foot, slightly to the West. Progressing anti-clockwise from the North round the skyline, the following features are observable: a building with a high, pointed roof; an open space with a range of hills in the distance; a small front garden; and a road passing in front of the house.

3 From the compass, note the orientation of the house, according to the position of the main entrance, to the nearest of the eight bearings: North, North-East, East, South-East, South, South-West, West, North-West. Mark this at the head of the geomantic chart at 'Orientation'.

The main entrance of 17 Hill Road is oriented between South-West and South, but closer to the South-West.

4 As described on page 19, try to identify the Dragon. 'True' Dragons are found only in a natural landscape, and consequently may not appear in an urban setting. In this case, 'false' dragons, in the forms of fountains,

confluences of water courses, or patterns in the ground, for example, may serve the purpose. If you cannot find a 'true' Dragon or a 'false' Dragon, identify the Tiger. Mark this, too, on the section of the geomantic chart headed 'Environmental Features'.

Ideally of course, for good *Feng Shui*, a building should be oriented towards the South, with the Dragon to the East and the Tiger to the West. Remember, however, that if your home or work-place has a different orientation, you should treat the entrance as if it were South-facing. In this way, you should look for the Dragon to the left and the Tiger to the right of the entrance, as you stand with your back to the building.

Sometimes, however, both the Dragon and the Tiger are obscured, in which case it will be necessary to try and identify the Black Tortoise (hills or buildings screening the back of the location) or the Red Bird (an open space with a single small projection) to the front.

John Mason's house is not detached. The presence of an adjoining wall means that no Dragon, 'true' or 'false', is discernible. Instead, the landscape needs to be examined for a Tiger prominence. Distant hills, at Chinese compass directions IX, 7 and X, are considered to be the Tiger.

5 The exterior observations have been completed, so that you can now move indoors.

Complete the 'Natal Number and Attributes' table on the geomantic chart by following the method given on page 87 (and in the example here).

John Mason's birth-date is 2nd January 1944. From the Table for the Dates of Chinese New Year given on page 102, it can be seen that John's date of birth occurred before the Chinese New Year in 1944. So the previous year, 1943, is taken as John's birth-year. 43 is divided by 9, to leave a remainder of 7. Subtracted from 10, this gives 3. So John's Annual Number is 3.

Placing the cursor over ring [M] of the Lo P'an at 2nd January, it can be seen from ring [G] that the Solar Fortnight Number for this date is 22.

From the Table of Solar Fortnights on page 104, in the column headed 'Male, Annual Number 3', alongside Solar

Fortnight 22 is the Natal Number 4.

From the Table of Natal Numbers and their Attributes on page 103, we see that the Natal Number 4 belongs to the trigram Sun: the type is Easterly; the direction, South-East; the polarity, Yin; and the Element, Wood.

6 Of the two orientation charts provided on the geomantic chart, select the one (either oriented to the four principal directions or the four 'corner' directions) which is most appropriate to the orientation of the building in question. Mark the position of the entrance in the appropriate side of the chart.

Now turn to the Table of the Eight Orientations of a Building and their Portent Numbers on page 105, and note the chart which matches the orientation of the building. Enter the figures representing the portents on the appropriate orientation chart.

17 Hill Road is oriented to the South-West, so the second chart is selected. The entrance is marked at the South-West position on the chart, and the remaining spaces are completed with the figures given for the South-West (K'un) type of building on the appropriate chart on page 105.

7 From the chart of the Natal Numbers and Attributes on your partially completed geomantic chart, note the Natal Element.

From the *productive* order of the Elements, given on page 89, keep a note of the Element which *produces* the Natal Element. Find this *productive* Element in the section headed 'Personal Direction' in the Table of Portents on the geomantic chart; and against this *productive* Element, mark a tick (meaning favourable) in the first column. From the *destructive* order of the Elements, given on page 89, note the Element which *destroys* the Natal Element. Find this Element in the Table of Portents on your geomantic chart; and against this *destructive* Element, mark a cross (meaning unfavourable), again in the first column. (Note that occasionally there may be more than one tick or cross. The Elements left unmarked signify neither favourable or unfavourable directions.)

John Mason's Natal Element has been found to be Wood. From the productive order of the Elements, shown on page 89, Wood is seen to be produced by Water, so a tick is placed in the blank column within the section headed 'Personal Direction' in the Table of Portents alongside Water in the first line.

From the destructive order of the Elements, Wood is seen to be destroyed by Metal, so a cross is marked in the blank column within the section headed 'Personal Direction' in the Table of Portents alongside Metal, in the seventh and eighth lines.

8 Enter the figures in the Orientation Chart into the Table of Portents at their appropriate directional places in the first narrow column of the section headed 'Building's Direction'. (Note that the Entrance is left blank.) From the list of portents on page 89, note the portents corresponding to the portent numbers marked in the Orientation Chart, and complete the Table of Portents accordingly, with ticks for auspicious directions and crosses for inauspicious ones, in the righthand column next to the 'Building's Direction' column. In the Summary column, note the total number of ticks and crosses marked for each direction.

In the case of John Mason's house, 'Entrance' will be marked in the South-West space. The figures in the Orientation Chart are then entered in the section headed 'Building's Direction' in the Table of Portents, and the table completed by reference to the list of portents on page 89.

9 Make a sketch map of the interior and exterior layout of the building in the space provided on the geomantic chart.

Study the Environmental Features chart which you have compiled. From your knowledge of auspicious and inauspicious features, note which are favourable and likely to stimulate beneficial *ch'i*, and those which are regarded as potentially harmful *sha*. Favourable features, for example, might include the Dragon, Bird, Tiger and Tortoise, and suitable flowing watercourses; while unfavourable features will include poles, pointed roofs and angles of building. Note these observations at the appropriate positions on your sketch map.

From John Mason's Environmental Chart, it can be seen that the Feng Shui of the house has both favourable and unfavourable features. No Dragon is visible, being hidden by the adjoining house. However, the Tiger – distant hills at Chinese compass directions IX, 7 and X – is auspicious, but the pointed roof of the house opposite, inauspicious. Each observation has been transferred to John Mason's sketch map in the appropriate position.

10 The next step is to decide how the rooms of the house can best be allocated, and suitable colour schemes incorporated.

In order to do this, three separate appraisals have to be made, the final recommendations being compiled when all factors have been balanced.

Firstly, the most suitable direction for the master bedroom should be established according to the horoscope of the owner, traditionally the male head of household. This is done by consulting the Table of Portents found on the geomantic chart and noting an orientation favourable for both the individual and for the building.

Secondly, it will be necessary to establish the most suitable bedrooms for the rest of the family, comparing these with the family relationships found in the Table of Trigrams on page 41.

The third step is to establish the suitability of rooms not yet designated according to the general qualities listed in the Table of Trigrams on page 41.

Note that the qualities associated with directions as found in the Table of Trigrams on page 41 may not always correspond to those found in the Building's Direction column of the Table of Portents on the geomantic chart. Personal judgement will therefore be important in deciding which rooms are appropriate in such instances, and any necessary *Feng Shui* adjustments made accordingly.

Suitable colour schemes may be chosen according to the direction each room faces, as described on page 45. Adverse *Feng Shui* situations are counterbalanced by using the colour which is associated with the Element *producing* the Element of the direction of the room.

In the geomantic chart for John Mason, from the Table of Portents, it appears that the most favourable direction for his bedroom, based on the horoscope, is the North. However, this is countered by the fact that, based on the orientation of the building, North is generally unfavourable, belonging to the portent 'Conclusion.' John Mason should therefore look for an orientation for his bedroom that will be compatible with his horoscope and the portents for the orientation of the building.

From the section headed 'Personal Direction' on the Table of Portents on John Mason's geomantic chart, the direction North-East is found to be neither favourable nor unfavourable, since neither a tick nor a cross has been marked. However, from the orientation of the house, the portent for North-East is found to be 'Vitality', which is highly favourable. This direction would therefore be excellent for everyone in the household, including John Mason.

Similarly, the directions East, South-East and South are also found to be neither favourable nor unfavourable for John Mason. However, they are each unfavourable generally, according to the portents for the building. Consequently, rooms facing these directions are not recommended for sustained use by John Mason or his family.

Both West and North-West are unfavourable for John Mason, as can again be seen by the crosses marked in the section headed 'Personal Direction'; but as far as the house is concerned, both directions have fortunate portents ('Celestial Physician' and 'Longevity'). These rooms could therefore be used by other members of the family to their advantage.

From a purely practical point-of-view, it would not be possible to use the small, North-East bedroom as the master bedroom. It would, however, be extremely favourable for the well-being and growth of the son, as the North-East trigram, Ken, (see page 41) represents 'Youngest Son.' In the Mason household, this would be suitable for the son, since he is the only boy and younger child.

John Mason and his wife will be obliged to use the double-bedroom in the South-West. This, being the entrance side, has no portents. However, by placing the bed in the North-East part of the room, they will benefit from the vitality of that particular orientation.

In considering the colour scheme for the master bedroom, as for other rooms, note is taken of the Element of the direction. In this case, the direction the bedroom faces is South-West; and from the Table of Portents on the geomantic chart, its Element is found to be Fire, so pink tones will be suitable.

The Western bedroom pertains to the trigram Tui, associated with the youngest daughter, and has the portent 7, 'Celestial Physician'. This placing would be extremely beneficial for the health of the daughter.

The bathroom is favourably placed in the North, the direction associated with Water.

According to the Eight Trigrams, the kitchen is unfavourably placed, since it is in the North, the direction associated with the Element Water, which destroys Fire, the operative Element of the kitchen. The optimum location for a kitchen, it will be remembered, is West. But it is not practicable to move the kitchen in this instance. Therefore, it might be expected that the geomancer would suggest placing a mirror on the South-East wall to reflect the favourable West direction. However, the North-West is also the direction of the pointed roof which, as you will see from the sketch map of John Mason's interior, is producing unfavourable sha. In this case, the mirror could be placed on the North wall where it will, at least, minimize the effect of the unfavourable North direction.

The house with the pointed roof, at direction XI, is regarded as extremely inauspicious, as pointed roofs represent the Element Fire, considered to be threatening when close to a residence.

It will be necessary to counterbalance this unfavourable Element. The pointed roof overlooks the kitchen. Therefore, the Lo P'an should be set up at the spot most under threat in the kitchen. With the Lo P'an placed so that the Rat is at North, the cursor is aligned with the highest point of the roof visible through the kitchen window. A straight edge or ruler is placed over the cursor, and the cursor rotated through 180°. Note is taken of the Element symbol at ring [H] on the side of the Lo P'an furthest away from the roof. This is seen to be the symbol for Metal.

In order to counteract the harmful Element of the pointed roof which is Fire, it is important to introduce the appropriate controlling Element of the Element under threat. This is found to be Earth, according to the productive sequence. Earth is represented by the colour yellow (see page 45). The geomancer would, therefore, suggest yellow decor as a possible remedy.

The dining-room, in the North-West, has the excellent portent, 'Celestial Physician', and is therefore favourable for the family generally. But from the attributes of the Eight Trigrams, it is clear that the dining-room – in the North-West (Kingship) –

and the living-room – in the South-West (Nourishment) – are situated contrarily. It would be inconvenient to exchange their positions, however, as this would put the dining-room far from the kitchen.

For this reason, the geomancer suggests placing the dining-table on the South-West side, and that the seating arrangements in the living-room should be centred round the North-West side.

When considering a colour scheme for the dining-room, from the Table of Portents on the geomantic chart, it is seen that the Element pertaining to the North-West is Metal. The colour associated with Metal is white (see page 45). However, white is considered to be a funereal colour and therefore unfavourable, so silver-grey tones would be more appropriate in the dining-room. Similarly, the Element of the South-West – the direction of the living-room – is known to be Fire. The colour associated with Fire is red. So pink tones would be appropriate, if red is thought to be too vibrant for the living-room.

Tables

TABLE 1

Dates of the Chinese New Year 1901–2000

The Chinese Year begins on a different date each year, coinciding with the second New Moon after the winter solstice.

19 Feb 1901 *Metal-Ox*	3 Feb 1916 *Fire-Dragon*	17 Feb 1931 *Metal-Sheep*	2 Feb 1946 *Fire-Dog*	15 Feb 1961 *Metal-Ox*	31 Jan 1976 *Fire-Dragon*	15 Feb 1991 *Metal-Sheep*
8 Feb 1902 *Water-Tiger*	23 Jan 1917 *Fire-Snake*	6 Feb 1932 *Water-Monkey*	22 Jan 1947 *Fire-Pig*	5 Feb 1962 *Water-Tiger*	18 Feb 1977 *Fire-Snake*	4 Feb 1992 *Water-Monkey*
29 Jan 1903 *Water-Hare*	11 Feb 1918 *Earth-Horse*	26 Jan 1933 *Water-Rooster*	10 Feb 1948 *Earth-Rat*	25 Jan 1963 *Water-Hare*	7 Feb 1978 *Earth-Horse*	23 Jan 1993 *Water-Rooster*
16 Feb 1904 *Wood-Dragon*	1 Feb 1919 *Earth-Sheep*	14 Feb 1934 *Wood-Dog*	29 Jan 1949 *Earth-Ox*	13 Feb 1964 *Wood-Dragon*	28 Jan 1979 *Earth-Sheep*	10 Feb 1994 *Wood-Dog*
4 Feb 1905 *Wood-Snake*	20 Feb 1920 *Metal-Monkey*	4 Feb 1935 *Wood-Pig*	17 Feb 1950 *Metal-Tiger*	2 Feb 1965 *Wood-Snake*	16 Feb 1980 *Metal-Monkey*	31 Jan 1995 *Wood-Pig*
25 Jan 1906 *Fire-Horse*	8 Feb 1921 *Metal-Rooster*	24 Jan 1936 *Fire-Rat*	6 Feb 1951 *Metal-Hare*	21 Jan 1966 *Fire-Horse*	5 Feb 1981 *Metal-Rooster*	19 Feb 1996 *Fire-Rat*
13 Feb 1907 *Fire-Sheep*	28 Jan 1922 *Water-Dog*	11 Feb 1937 *Fire-Ox*	27 Jan 1952 *Water-Dragon*	9 Feb 1967 *Fire-Sheep*	25 Jan 1982 *Water-Dog*	7 Feb 1997 *Fire-Ox*
2 Feb 1908 *Earth-Monkey*	16 Feb 1923 *Water-Pig*	31 Jan 1938 *Earth-Tiger*	14 Feb 1953 *Water-Snake*	30 Jan 1968 *Earth-Monkey*	13 Feb 1983 *Water-Pig*	28 Jan 1998 *Earth-Tiger*
22 Jan 1909 *Earth-Rooster*	5 Feb 1924 *Wood-Rat*	19 Feb 1939 *Earth-Hare*	3 Feb 1954 *Wood-Horse*	17 Feb 1969 *Earth-Rooster*	2 Feb 1984 *Wood-Rat*	16 Feb 1999 *Earth-Hare*
10 Feb 1910 *Metal-Dog*	25 Jan 1925 *Wood-Ox*	8 Feb 1940 *Metal-Dragon*	24 Jan 1955 *Wood-Sheep*	6 Feb 1970 *Metal-Dog*	20 Feb 1985 *Wood-Ox*	5 Feb 2000 *Metal-Dragon*
30 Jan 1911 *Metal-Pig*	13 Feb 1926 *Fire-Tiger*	27 Jan 1941 *Metal-Snake*	12 Feb 1956 *Fire-Monkey*	27 Jan 1971 *Metal-Pig*	9 Feb 1986 *Fire-Tiger*	
18 Feb 1912 *Water-Rat*	2 Feb 1927 *Fire-Hare*	15 Feb 1942 *Water-Horse*	31 Jan 1957 *Fire-Rooster*	15 Feb 1972 *Water-Rat*	29 Jan 1987 *Fire-Hare*	
6 Feb 1913 *Water-Ox*	23 Jan 1928 *Earth-Dragon*	5 Feb 1943 *Water-Sheep*	18 Feb 1958 *Earth-Dog*	3 Feb 1973 *Water-Ox*	17 Feb 1988 *Earth-Dragon*	
26 Jan 1914 *Wood-Tiger*	10 Feb 1929 *Earth-Snake*	25 Jan 1944 *Wood-Monkey*	8 Feb 1959 *Earth-Pig*	23 Jan 1974 *Wood-Tiger*	6 Feb 1989 *Earth-Snake*	
14 Feb 1915 *Wood-Hare*	30 Jan 1930 *Metal-Horse*	13 Feb 1945 *Wood-Rooster*	28 Jan 1960 *Metal-Rat*	11 Feb 1975 *Wood-Hare*	27 Jan 1990 *Metal-Horse*	

TABLE 2

Code Numbers for the Years 1901–2000

Year	1901	1902	1903	1904	1905	1906	1907	1908	1909	1910	1911	1912	1913	1914	1915	1916	1917	1918	1919	1920
Code	15	20	25	30	36	41	46	51	57	2	7	12	18	23	28	33	39	44	49	54

Year	1921	1922	1923	1924	1925	1926	1927	1928	1929	1930	1931	1932	1933	1934	1935	1936	1937	1938	1939	1940
Code	0	5	10	15	21	26	31	36	42	47	52	57	3	8	13	18	24	29	34	39

Year	1941	1942	1943	1944	1945	1946	1947	1948	1949	1950	1951	1952	1953	1954	1955	1956	1957	1958	1959	1960
Code	45	50	55	0	6	11	16	21	27	32	37	42	48	53	58	3	9	14	19	24

Year	1961	1962	1963	1964	1965	1966	1967	1968	1969	1970	1971	1972	1973	1974	1975	1976	1977	1978	1979	1980
Code	30	35	40	45	51	56	1	6	12	17	22	27	33	38	43	48	54	59	4	9

Year	1981	1982	1983	1984	1985	1986	1987	1988	1989	1990	1991	1992	1993	1994	1995	1996	1997	1998	1999	2000
Code	15	20	25	30	36	41	46	51	57	2	7	12	18	23	28	33	39	44	49	54

TABLE 3

Table of Natal Numbers and their Attributes

Natal Number	Trigram	Type	Direction	Polarity	Element
1	*K'an*	Easterly	N	*Yang*	Water
2	*K'un*	Westerly	SW	*Yin*	Earth
3	*Chen*	Easterly	E	*Yang*	Wood
4	*Sun*	Easterly	SE	*Yin*	Wood
5 (m)	*Ken*	Westerly	NE	*Yang*	Earth
5 (f)	*K'un*	Westerly	SW	*Yin*	Earth
6	*Ch'ien*	Westerly	NW	*Yang*	Metal
7	*Tui*	Westerly	W	*Yin*	Metal
8	*Ken*	Westerly	NE	*Yang*	Earth
9	*Li*	Easterly	S	*Yin*	Fire

TABLE 4

The Twenty-four Solar Fortnights and their Natal Numbers

		MALE			FEMALE		
		ANNUAL NUMBER					
		1	2	3	1	2	3
		4	5	6	4	5	6
		7	8	9	7	8	9
SOLAR FORTNIGHT NUMBER	NAMES OF THE SOLAR FORTNIGHTS	NATAL NUMBER					
1	Spring begins	8	2	5	7	4	1
2	Rain water	8	2	5	7	4	1
3	Insects awaken	7	1	4	8	5	2
4	Spring equinox	7	1	4	8	5	2
5	Clear and bright	6	9	3	9	6	3
6	Corn rain	6	9	3	9	6	3
7	Summer begins	5	8	2	1	7	4
8	Corn sprouting	5	8	2	1	7	4
9	Corn in ear	4	7	1	2	8	5
10	Summer solstice	4	7	1	2	8	5
11	Little heat	3	6	9	3	9	6
12	Great heat	3	6	9	3	9	6
13	Autumn begins	2	5	8	4	1	7
14	Heat ends	2	5	8	4	1	7
15	White dew	1	4	7	5	2	8
16	Autumn equinox	1	4	7	5	2	8
17	Cold dew	9	3	6	6	3	9
18	Frost descends	9	3	6	6	3	9
19	Winter begins	8	2	5	7	4	1
20	Little snow	8	2	5	7	4	1
21	Great snow	7	1	4	8	5	2
22	Winter solstice	7	1	4	8	5	2
23	Little cold	6	9	3	9	6	3
24	Great cold	6	9	3	9	6	3

TABLE 5

The Eight Orientations of a Building and their Portent Numbers

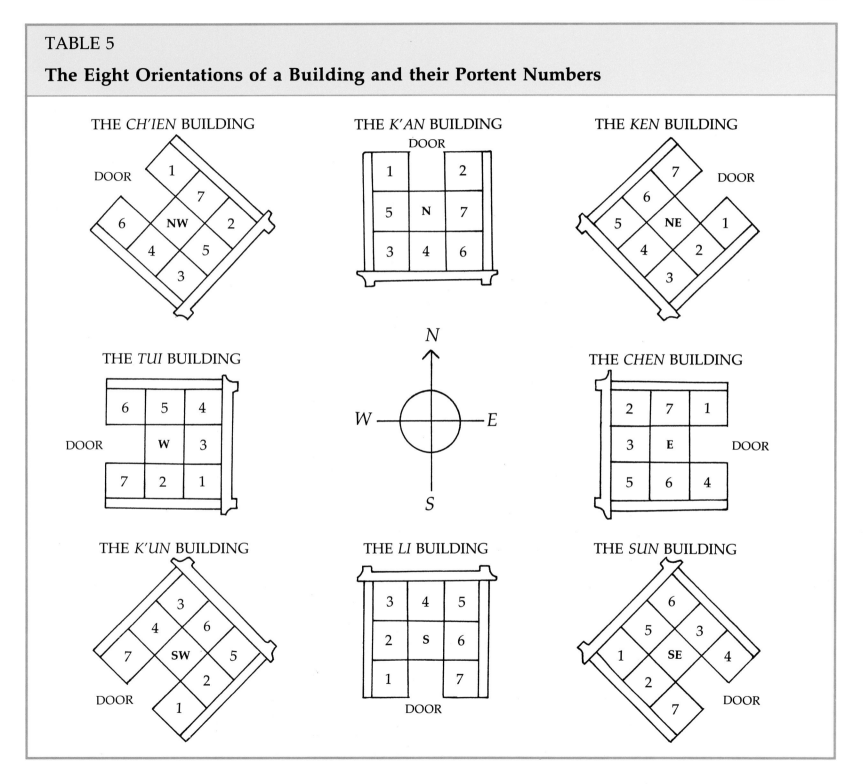

TABLE 6

Sequences of Stems and Branches

The following table lists the sixty possible combinations of Heavenly Stems and Earthly Branches, together with their popular Element – Animal names. (Note that even-numbered Stems are always paired with even-numbered Branches, and odd Stems with odd Branches.)

Number of Stem and Branch Combination	Stem–Branch	Element–Animal	Number of Stem and Branch Combination	Stem–Branch	Element–Animal
1	1 – I	Wood–Rat	31	1 – VII	Wood–Horse
2	2 – II	Wood–Ox	32	2 – VIII	Wood–Sheep
3	3 – III	Fire–Tiger	33	3 – IX	Fire–Monkey
4	4 – IV	Fire–Hare	34	4 – X	Fire–Rooster
5	5 – V	Earth–Dragon	35	5 – XI	Earth–Dog
6	6 – VI	Earth–Snake	36	6 – XII	Earth–Pig
7	7 – VII	Metal–Horse	37	7 – I	Metal–Rat
8	8 – VIII	Metal–Sheep	38	8 – II	Metal–Ox
9	9 – IX	Water–Monkey	39	9 – III	Water–Tiger
10	10 – X	Water–Rooster	40	10 – IV	Water–Hare
11	1 – XI	Wood–Dog	41	1 – V	Wood–Dragon
12	2 – XII	Wood–Pig	42	2 – VI	Wood–Snake
13	3 – I	Fire–Rat	43	3 – VII	Fire–Horse
14	4 – II	Fire–Ox	44	4 – VIII	Fire–Sheep
15	5 – III	Earth–Tiger	45	5 – IX	Earth–Monkey
16	6 – IV	Earth–Hare	46	6 – X	Earth–Rooster
17	7 – V	Metal–Dragon	47	7 – XI	Metal–Dog
18	8 – VI	Metal–Snake	48	8 – XII	Metal–Pig
19	9 – VII	Water–Horse	49	9 – I	Water–Rat
20	10 – VIII	Water–Sheep	50	10 – II	Water–Ox
21	1 – IX	Wood–Monkey	51	1 – III	Wood–Tiger
22	2 – X	Wood–Rooster	52	2 – IV	Wood–Hare
23	3 – XI	Fire–Dog	53	3 – V	Fire–Dragon
24	4 – XII	Fire–Pig	54	4 – VI	Fire–Snake
25	5 – I	Earth–Rat	55	5 – VII	Earth–Horse
26	6 – II	Earth–Ox	56	6 – VIII	Earth–Sheep
27	7 – III	Metal–Tiger	57	7 – IX	Metal–Monkey
28	8 – IV	Metal–Hare	58	8 – X	Metal–Rooster
29	9 – V	Water–Dragon	59	9 – XI	Water–Dog
30	10 – VI	Water–Snake	60	10 – XII	Water–Pig

TABLE 7

Stem and Branch Codes

Code								Code						
1	Jan 1	Mar 2	May 1	Jun 30	Aug 29	Oct 28	Dec 27	31	Jan 31	Apr 1	May 31	Jul 30	Sep 28	Nov 27
2	Jan 2	Mar 3	May 2	Jul 1	Aug 30	Oct 29	Dec 28	32	Feb 1	Apr 2	Jun 1	Jul 31	Sep 29	Nov 28
3	Jan 3	Mar 4	May 3	Jul 2	Aug 31	Oct 30	Dec 29	33	Feb 2	Apr 3	Jun 2	Aug 1	Sep 30	Nov 29
4	Jan 4	Mar 5	May 4	Jul 3	Sep 1	Oct 31	Dec 30	34	Feb 3	Apr 4	Jun 3	Aug 2	Oct 1	Nov 30
5	Jan 5	Mar 6	May 5	Jul 4	Sep 2	Nov 1	Dec 31	35	Feb 4	Apr 5	Jun 4	Aug 3	Oct 2	Dec 1
6	Jan 6	Mar 7	May 6	Jul 5	Sep 3	Nov 2		36	Feb 5	Apr 6	Jun 5	Aug 4	Oct 3	Dec 2
7	Jan 7	Mar 8	May 7	Jul 6	Sep 4	Nov 3		37	Feb 6	Apr 7	Jun 6	Aug 5	Oct 4	Dec 3
8	Jan 8	Mar 9	May 8	Jul 7	Sep 5	Nov 4		38	Feb 7	Apr 8	Jun 7	Aug 6	Oct 5	Dec 4
9	Jan 9	Mar 10	May 9	Jul 8	Sep 6	Nov 5		39	Feb 8	Apr 9	Jun 8	Aug 7	Oct 6	Dec 5
10	Jan 10	Mar 11	May 10	Jul 9	Sep 7	Nov 6		40	Feb 9	Apr 10	Jun 9	Aug 8	Oct 7	Dec 6
11	Jan 11	Mar 12	May 11	Jul 10	Sep 8	Nov 7		41	Feb 10	Apr 11	Jun 10	Aug 9	Oct 8	Dec 7
12	Jan 12	Mar 13	May 12	Jul 11	Sep 9	Nov 8		42	Feb 11	Apr 12	Jun 11	Aug 10	Oct 9	Dec 8
13	Jan 13	Mar 14	May 13	Jul 12	Sep 10	Nov 9		43	Feb 12	Apr 13	Jun 12	Aug 11	Oct 10	Dec 9
14	Jan 14	Mar 15	May 14	Jul 13	Sep 11	Nov 10		44	Feb 13	Apr 14	Jun 13	Aug 12	Oct 11	Dec 10
15	Jan 15	Mar 16	May 15	Jul 14	Sep 12	Nov 11		45	Feb 14	Apr 15	Jun 14	Aug 13	Oct 12	Dec 11
16	Jan 16	Mar 17	May 16	Jul 15	Sep 13	Nov 12		46	Feb 15	Apr 16	Jun 15	Aug 14	Oct 13	Dec 12
17	Jan 17	Mar 18	May 17	Jul 16	Sep 14	Nov 13		47	Feb 16	Apr 17	Jun 16	Aug 15	Oct 14	Dec 13
18	Jan 18	Mar 19	May 18	Jul 17	Sep 15	Nov 14		48	Feb 17	Apr 18	Jun 17	Aug 16	Oct 15	Dec 14
19	Jan 19	Mar 20	May 19	Jul 18	Sep 16	Nov 15		49	Feb 18	Apr 19	Jun 18	Aug 17	Oct 16	Dec 15
20	Jan 20	Mar 21	May 20	Jul 19	Sep 17	Nov 16		50	Feb 19	Apr 20	Jun 19	Aug 18	Oct 17	Dec 16
21	Jan 21	Mar 22	May 21	Jul 20	Sep 18	Nov 17		51	Feb 20	Apr 21	Jun 20	Aug 19	Oct 18	Dec 17
22	Jan 22	Mar 23	May 22	Jul 21	Sep 19	Nov 18		52	Feb 21	Apr 22	Jun 21	Aug 20	Oct 19	Dec 18
23	Jan 23	Mar 24	May 23	Jul 22	Sep 20	Nov 19		53	Feb 22	Apr 23	Jun 22	Aug 21	Oct 20	Dec 19
24	Jan 24	Mar 25	May 24	Jul 23	Sep 21	Nov 20		54	Feb 23	Apr 24	Jun 23	Aug 22	Oct 21	Dec 20
25	Jan 25	Mar 26	May 25	Jul 24	Sep 22	Nov 21		55	Feb 24	Apr 25	Jun 24	Aug 23	Oct 22	Dec 21
26	Jan 26	Mar 27	May 26	Jul 25	Sep 23	Nov 22		56	Feb 25	Apr 26	Jun 25	Aug 24	Oct 23	Dec 22
27	Jan 27	Mar 28	May 27	Jul 26	Sep 24	Nov 23		57	Feb 26	Apr 27	Jun 26	Aug 25	Oct 24	Dec 23
28	Jan 28	Mar 29	May 28	Jul 27	Sep 25	Nov 24		58	Feb 27	Apr 28	Jun 27	Aug 26	Oct 25	Dec 24
29	Jan 29	Mar 30	May 29	Jul 28	Sep 26	Nov 25		59	Feb 28	Apr 29	Jun 28	Aug 27	Oct 26	Dec 25
30	Jan 30	Mar 31	May 30	Jul 29	Sep 27	Nov 26		60	Mar 1	Apr 30	Jun 29	Aug 28	Oct 27	Dec 26

Geomantic Chart

Name _____ *John Mason*

Date of Birth _____ *2nd January 1944*

Family _____ *Laura (wife)*

Carol (daughter)

Paul (son)

Building _____ *17 Hill Road*

Orientation _____ *South-West*

NATAL NUMBER AND ATTRIBUTES

Natal number	*4*
Trigram	*Sun*
Type	*East*
Direction	*S.E.*
Polarity	*Yin*
Natal Element	*Wood*

ORIENTATION CHARTS

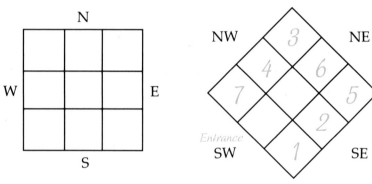

TABLE OF PORTENTS

Personal Direction				Building's Direction		Summary
N	☵	Water	✓	*3*	*Conclusion* X	✓ X
NE	☶	Earth		*6*	*Vitality* ✓	✓
E	☳	Wood		*5*	*Disaster* X	X
SE	☴	Wood		*2*	*Seven imps* X	X
S	☲	Fire		*1*	*Six ghosts* X	X
SW	☷	Fire			*Entrance*	
W	☱	Metal	X	*7*	*Celestial Ph.* ✓	✓ X
NW	☰	Metal	X	*4*	*Longevity* ✓	✓ X

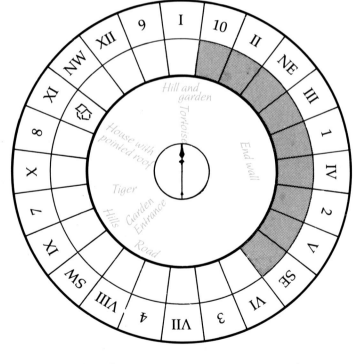

ENVIRONMENTAL FEATURES

FENG SHUI PLAN – UPPER FLOOR

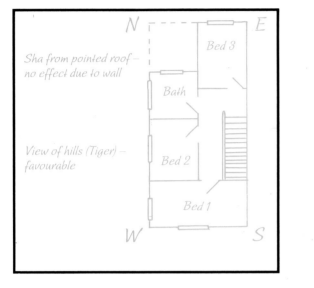

FENG SHUI PLAN – LOWER FLOOR

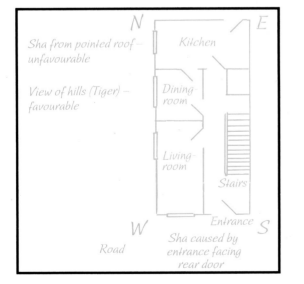

GEOMANCER'S RECOMMENDATIONS

Place dragon picture or ornament on the interior Eastern wall, which obscures the Dragon in the landscape.

As the entrance faces the stairs, a bead curtain should be hung between them to counteract unfavourable sha.

The open space in front of the house is favourable, but could be improved by a token pond or bird-bath.

Ground floor: the disposition of the rooms is not entirely satisfactory. Place a mirror on the North wall of the kitchen to reflect harmonious influences from the South. The unfavourable effect of the pointed roof may be deflected by the yellow tones in the kitchen decor.

Ideally, the positions of living-room and dining-room should be exchanged. However, as this is not practical, place the dining-table near the South-West side of room, and ensure yellow tints predominate. In the living-room, place chairs at the North-West, and introduce a pink/grey colour scheme, in addition to indoor plants.

In the main bedroom, place the bed in the North-East corner. John Mason should store clothes and personal possessions to the North of the room; his wife to have hers in the South-West, in accordance with the trigram for mother. Decorate in pink tones.

Geomantic Chart

Name _____

Date of Birth _____

Family _____

_____

Building _____

Orientation _____

NATAL NUMBER AND ATTRIBUTES

Natal number	
Trigram	
Type	
Direction	
Polarity	
Natal Element	

ORIENTATION CHARTS

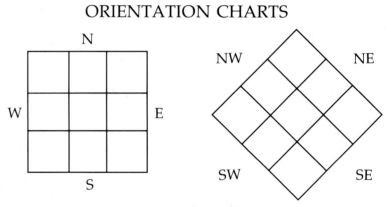

TABLE OF PORTENTS

Personal Direction			Building's Direction	Summary
N	☵	Water		
NE	☶	Earth		
E	☳	Wood		
SE	☴	Wood		
S	☲	Fire		
SW	☷	Fire		
W	☱	Metal		
NW	☰	Metal		

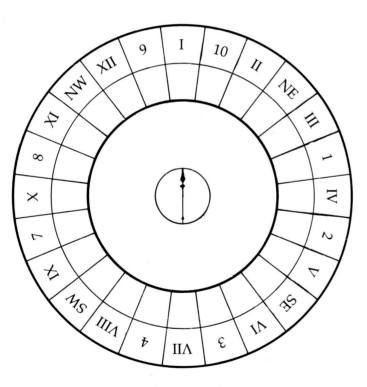

ENVIRONMENTAL FEATURES

FENG SHUI PLAN – UPPER FLOOR

GEOMANCER'S RECOMMENDATIONS

FENG SHUI PLAN – LOWER FLOOR

Index